Italian Fascism, 1914–1945

Claudia Baldoli

Italian Fascism, 1914–1945

Themes and Interpretations

Claudia Baldoli
Dipartimento di Studi Storici
University of Milan
Milan, Italy

ISBN 978-3-031-41903-4   ISBN 978-3-031-41904-1 (eBook)
https://doi.org/10.1007/978-3-031-41904-1

© The Editor(s) (if applicable) and The Author(s), under exclusive licence to Springer Nature Switzerland AG 2023
This work is subject to copyright. All rights are solely and exclusively licensed by the Publisher, whether the whole or part of the material is concerned, specifically the rights of translation, reprinting, reuse of illustrations, recitation, broadcasting, reproduction on microfilms or in any other physical way, and transmission or information storage and retrieval, electronic adaptation, computer software, or by similar or dissimilar methodology now known or hereafter developed.
The use of general descriptive names, registered names, trademarks, service marks, etc. in this publication does not imply, even in the absence of a specific statement, that such names are exempt from the relevant protective laws and regulations and therefore free for general use.
The publisher, the authors, and the editors are safe to assume that the advice and information in this book are believed to be true and accurate at the date of publication. Neither the publisher nor the authors or the editors give a warranty, expressed or implied, with respect to the material contained herein or for any errors or omissions that may have been made. The publisher remains neutral with regard to jurisdictional claims in published maps and institutional affiliations.

This Palgrave Macmillan imprint is published by the registered company Springer Nature Switzerland AG.
The registered company address is: Gewerbestrasse 11, 6330 Cham, Switzerland

Paper in this product is recyclable.

Contents

1	**Introduction**	1
	References	4
2	**The Origins of Fascism: Contemporary Interpretations**	5
	The Historical Context	5
	Fascism: "Son of the War"	5
	Post-war Italy: from the "Red Biennial" to the "Black Biennial"	9
	Contemporary Interpretations	15
	The First Coup: 1915	16
	Fascism as the Armed Reaction of Capitalism	18
	The Mistakes of the Italian Left	20
	"Autobiography of the Nation": Fascism as a Revelation of Italian History	24
	The Crisis of the Liberal State	28
	Autobiography of Fascism	30
	An "Anti-Party"?	32
	Making Sense of Mussolini	34
	References	36
3	**Coming to Terms with the Near Past: Post-war Historiography**	39
	Post-war Research on the Origins of Fascism	40
	Renzo De Felice's Biography of Mussolini and Its Impact:	
	The Early Years	44
	The Question of Consensus	48
	A Totalitarian regime? The Origins of a Long-term Debate	49
	The Conquest of Power	51
	Fascist Culture and Ideology	52
	The First Studies on Fascist Colonialism	56
	The Controversies in the 1970s and 1980s	58
	References	59

4	**The Historiography of Fascism from the End of the Cold War**	63
	New Research on the Origins of Fascism	66
	War, Post-war and Political Violence	66
	Beyond Violence: What was the First Fascism?	72
	Reassessing Mussolini	74
	New Studies on the Regime	77
	A Fascist Economy?	77
	Racism and Colonialism	80
	The Regime's Foreign Policy	83
	The Fascist Wars	85
	Reconsidering the Consensus	89
	Centre and Periphery, State and Party	93
	A Fascist Welfare State?	94
	Women in the Fascist Regime	95
	The Catholic Church	97
	References	98
5	**The Italian Social Republic (1943–1945): Historiography on Fascism's Final Years**	103
	A "Civil War"	105
	The RSI as Part of the History of Italian Fascism	106
	References	109
6	**Conclusion**	111
	References	114
	Index	115

CHAPTER 1

Introduction

The numerous events organised around Italy for the centenary of the march on Rome in 2022 (seminars, conferences, book launches, interviews) have prompted historians to discuss the latest research and interpretations not only on the origins of fascism, but also on the establishment of the dictatorship, on the relationship between violence, repression, and consensus, and on the military core of the movement, the regime, and its ideology. Some of the events also raised the question as to whether Italy has yet confronted its fascist past 100 years later, especially as elections in September brought to power Giorgia Meloni and her party *Fratelli d'Italia* ("Brothers of Italy", heir to the neo-fascist party *Movimento Sociale Italiano*—Italian Social Movement, MSI—, founded in 1946)—the only parliamentary opposition by 2022 to the unelected, liberal banker Mario Draghi.

While this book does not discuss politics in Italy today, it aims to portray the ways in which "historical" fascism—that is to say, fascism between 1922 and 1945—has been interpreted both by its contemporaries and by historians from 1945 until today. The object is to try to explain a paradox: on the one hand, an extremely rich historiography has produced thorough research on many of the aspects and complexities of fascism; on the other hand, at the level of public opinion, fuelled by the media, simplified and distorted views (that imply a denial of the brutal and violent aspects of the fascist movement and regime) are still predominant.

Historians have investigated the history of the regime by studying its own propaganda (architecture, education, the cult of the leader); the daily life of Italians, and the extent and limits of the consensus; the role of violence in its establishment and throughout its duration, both within Italy and in the colonies; the importance of a military culture and involvement in war (from the repression of Libyan resistance in the 1920s to the final defeat in the Second World War in 1943) for most of its existence. At the same time, popular magazines and TV documentaries have since the 1950s propagated a superficial

© The Author(s), under exclusive license to Springer Nature Switzerland AG 2023
C. Baldoli, *Italian Fascism, 1914-1945*,
https://doi.org/10.1007/978-3-031-41904-1_1

image of a benevolent dictatorship, without providing any evidence (Baldassini 2008). In the 1990s, with the end of the Cold War and the system of political parties that was established after 1945, the extreme right was able to return to power for the first time, in coalition with media magnate Silvio Berlusconi who, followed years later by Northern League leader Matteo Salvini, repeatedly expressed his appreciation for fascism. In December 2022, having to confront accusations that some of her ministers were philo-fascists and apologists for the MSI, prime minister Meloni claimed to have no connections with fascism and repudiated Benito Mussolini's anti-Semitic laws of 1938, but argued that the MSI had played a positive role in Italian democracy, having led the "defeated ones" to democracy and having fought violence and terrorism. In fact, although the party had indeed taken part in Italian elections, many of the MSI's founders and members had played important roles in Mussolini's Social Republic of 1943–1945, including support for its racist and antisemitic ideology, which they defended well into the 1980s (Parlato in Resta and Zeno-Zencovich, 2015, p. 148); moreover, some of them were linked with groups, like *Ordine Nuovo*, that were implicated in neo-fascist terrorist atrocities between 1969 and 1980. The party was, therefore, largely foreign to democracy, as historians of the post-war Italian right have demonstrated (for example, Tarchi 1995; Germinario 2001). It is thus evident that there exists a schism between the results of historical research and ideas about fascism conveyed by a section of the political class and the media.

As John Foot reminds us in one of the many books on fascism published in 2022, Italian fascism was not a "necessary evil". Moreover, violence was an essential ingredient throughout, and it did not bring order and stability, but ended in war and civil war. It also enabled the rise of Nazism in Germany and other right-wing authoritarian regimes (Foot 2022, p. 6). The dark reality of fascism was sometimes obscured by the attention paid to its architecture, the most visible sign of its legacy in Italian cities today, an outcome revealed by a collective project on the sites of fascist memory that produced a website and a book (https://www.luoghifascismo.it/; Albanese and Ceci, 2022). During the first public discussion of that project, held in Milan in November, Paolo Pezzino, a historian of Nazi retaliation and atrocities in Italy in 1943–1945, stressed the importance of the historian's work in spreading a factually correct knowledge of Italian fascism to help avoid the risk of its return. It seems implausible to think that fascism could re-establish itself in the same way as it did in 1922, but it could reappear under different guises, so that discussion of historiography is much needed if we want to know what fascism actually did to Italian (and colonial) society. A critical and intelligent public opinion, necessary for building a responsible citizenship, can only be based on knowledge of the historical research and debates.

This book was also prompted by many years of teaching modern Italian history, including specific courses on fascism, in British universities. The subject attracted genuine interest, both in quantitative terms (the courses were always fully subscribed) and in terms of the quality of seminar discussions, which made the teaching experience lively and engaged. This was partly made possible by the existence of a high-quality literature on fascism in the English language, some of which was translated from the Italian. However, a large part of the historiographical debate in Italian was not, for language reasons, accessible to the students. I cannot recall how many times students asked me where they could read about a specific historian's work, or a discussion on a distinctive aspect, since they were unfortunately not available in English. Sometimes questions concerned anti-fascist intellectuals who lived under the regime: apart from Antonio Gramsci and a few famous figures, most had not been translated, making it difficult to understand the complexity of contemporary interpretations. Who were, for example, Luigi Salvatorelli or Guido Dorso, and what did they argue? How did the communist interpretation of fascism develop and differ from the socialist, catholic, democratic and liberal interpretations? What impact did these have on post-1945 historiography? How much was historiography influenced by politics in the post-war years? Why was there an attempt by the media to portray fascism as a benevolent regime and how did historians respond? What were the most important results of the historical research from the 1970s and 1980s? And how did the generation of historians who emerged after the end of the Cold War complicate the picture in terms of new interpretations, approaches and subjects of study? How did they engage with previous debates and research?

This book seeks to address all these questions by presenting works that have not been translated, not only for the benefit of English-speaking university students of Italian fascism, but also for non-Italian speakers who are interested in the historiography of fascism in general. I have sometimes included translated books, or works that first appeared in English, when they have had a particular importance in shaping a specific debate among Italian historians, or when they have been referred to and cited as seminal in Italian historiography. However, the discussion is mostly based on historians whose works have not been translated, but which are often cited in English-language books: for example, "what has this Mario Isnenghi written on fascist culture?" was one of the typical questions I was asked. This is not, therefore, a book on the history of Italian fascism, but on its Italian historiography, although it contextualises the debates within the different historical periods under scrutiny.

Inevitably, the book is based on a selection and does not attempt to be comprehensive, but I hope that it will nonetheless be a contribution to the understanding of a rich and ever-developing debate, and that it can be a useful tool in English-language classes on Italian fascism. The book is the result of many years of research and regular participation in conferences and seminars on Italian fascism, and I am grateful to so many historians that it would be impossible to list them all: many are authors of works I discuss here, or former teachers, former fellow-students, colleagues. I also wish to thank the students who participated in my courses on Italian fascism at the universities of London and Newcastle: this book has grown with them, too—and with them in mind.

REFERENCES

Albanese, Giulia, Ceci, Lucia (eds), *I luoghi del fascismo. Memoria, politica, rimozione* (Rome: Viella, 2022).

Baldassini, Cristina, *L'ombra di Mussolini. L'Italia moderata e la memoria del fascismo: 1945–1960* (Soveria Mannelli: Rubbettino, 2008).

Foot, John, *Gli anni neri. Ascesa e caduta del fascismo* (Rome-Bari: Laterza, 2022; English ed. 2022).

Germinario, Francesco, *Estranei alla democrazia. Negazionismo e antisemitismo nella destra radicale italiana* (Pisa: BFS, 2001).

Resta, Giorgio, Zeno-Zencovich, Vincenzo, *Leggi razziali. Passato, presente* (Rome: Roma Tre Press, 2015).

Tarchi, Marco, *Esuli in patria. I fascisti nell'Italia repubblicana* (Parma: Guanda, 1995).

CHAPTER 2

The Origins of Fascism: Contemporary Interpretations

The Historical Context

This chapter will explore the interpretations of fascism attempted during its own lifetime: from the foundation of the fascist movement in 1919 until the end of the Second World War, historians, intellectuals, and political protagonists sought to understand how fascism rose to power. Before venturing into an analysis of this very first historiography, the chapter provides the historical context for the origins of fascism in the First World War and the post-war years.

Fascism: "Son of the War"

At the start of the Second World War, the historian and fascist Gioacchino Volpe explained, in a book on Italian society during the first global conflict, the intransigent rejection of war propagated by the peasant unions: "No party that wanted the peasants on their side … could talk about war. Because if the Libyan conflict, with even a vague prospect of land to be conquered and some religious colouring found them not too ill-disposed, the current war left them indifferent." (Volpe 1992, p. 91). Another historian, the anti-fascist exile Gaetano Salvemini, writing one of his lectures for Harvard University during the Second World War, reached a similar conclusion: for the Italian people, "intervention in war was nothing else than the result of an extravagant perversity of the political leaders". Those who promoted Italy's entry into the First World War were only supported by a minority of the population. "In the cities and in the countryside the masses of workers supported either the socialists or the catholics and were in favour of neutrality". (Salvemini 1979, p. 110). The reflections of Volpe and Salvemini, though from opposing sides of the political spectrum, were based on an objective observation of Italian attitudes to the First World War in 1914–1915. Antimilitarism was particularly widespread in the countryside, where there were continual demonstrations against war between August 1914 and the Italian intervention in May 1915. The mass pacifist mobilisation was evident also in rural areas near cities where interventionism prevailed, to the extent that those months can be regarded as "an empirical referendum, certainly not requested by the government but practiced by the country." (Cammarano 2015, p. 2).

Prefects' reports from all over Italy described how neutralist demonstrations were much more numerous and better organised than those of the interventionists. However, from February 1915, the interventionist minority began to respond with demonstrations of their own across the country (Isnenghi 1994, p. 212). Not only was the interventionist movement a minority, but it was also divided within itself. Democratic interventionists saw the conflict as an opportunity to complete the wars of national unification, in the hope of annexing from Austrian Empire the "unredeemed lands" of Trentino and South Tyrol and Friuli Venezia Giulia, as well as defeating Italy's "historic" Habsburg enemy; despite the presence of Tzarist Russia on the side of the Entente, democratic interventionists also described the war as a defence of democracy against the absolutist powers of Germany and Austria.

Nationalist interventionists, on the contrary, were hoping that Italy's participation in the war would result in territorial gains beyond the Italian lands occupied by Austria, particularly the extension of Italian power into the Balkans, starting with Dalmatia. The jurist (and later fascist minister of justice) Alfredo Rocco, and many other nationalists, regarded war as a necessity for Italy to expand in the world. They believed that, as a poor country, Italy had a right even to territories occupied by other powers that they regarded as decadent, like France—although their over-inflated evaluation of Italy's military capacities did not lead to a realistic expansion programme. They were anti-democratic and, with the futurist vanguard, among the most vocal opponents of the liberal state represented by Giovanni Giolitti (five times prime minister before fascism seized power), socialism and the parliamentary system, which they considered to be obstacles between the nation and the state, an obstruction to the participation of new generations in national politics. In 1909 the writer Filippo Tommaso Marinetti had published the Manifesto of Futurism, which exalted modernity, speed, war, anti-socialism, and anti-feminism. In fact, these radical nationalists and futurists remained a minority of intellectuals, incapable of competing with either socialist or catholic organisations. It was only participation in the war that allowed them to mobilise the middle classes in political terms (Gentile 1999, pp. 184–5; 23–24). Nationalism and futurism shared the myth of the will to power, hostility to egalitarianism and humanitarianism, contempt for parliament, a conception of politics as an activity for shaping the consciousness of the masses, the cult of youth as a new leading aristocracy, apology for violence, and direct action. The most influential expression of the new radical nationalism was the hostility displayed towards Giolitti by intellectual circles such as those around the journal *La Voce* (Gentile 2002, pp. 5–15).

All interventionists took from the Mazzinian tradition (from the republican Giuseppe Mazzini, 1805–1872) the vision of the Risorgimento (the movement for the unification of Italy in the nineteenth century) as an "unfinished revolution" which had failed to accomplish the nationalisation of the masses. Sociologically, this anti-Giolittian opposition was pursued chiefly by young people from the petit bourgeoisie, who were joined by nationalist intellectuals who wanted an anti-socialist and anti-democratic reaction, and who had already elaborated a project for the authoritarian transformation of the state in order to pursue a politics of national power and imperialist expansion. The interventionism of the anti-Giolittian intellectuals originated from this heterogeneous spirit of revolt.

The deep divide between neutralists and interventionists widened as the war progressed and often appeared as a form of civil war within the wider conflict. Dissatisfaction with the wartime economic situation, especially the government-imposed food restrictions, grew among the rural population in 1917. The cost of living had increased by almost 90% from 1915, while subsidies to soldiers' families had remained unchanged until May 1917, when they were subject to paltry increases. Moreover, the number of soldiers who had to maintain a family grew, since in January 1917 those born in 1874 were called up—generally 40-year-old peasants already worn out by work and with many children. The economic hardships favoured the "defeatist" campaign, which had an impact both on the home front and among soldiers. Prefects from all the Italian provinces wrote to the ministry of interior that anti-war sentiments were spreading, particularly among the peasantry. To local authorities it was unacceptable that, instead of understanding the "noble" reasons that had led to the wartime limitations of bread and flour, the peasants refused to cooperate. As with the women who protested over inadequate war subsidies, the peasants seemed to be influenced by socialist or catholic propaganda. Although any mass initiatives could be easily repressed by the police, prefects warned that there were symptoms of a developing anti-war public spirit.

Particularly after the October 1917 defeat of the Italian army at Caporetto (the town in present-day Slovenia where the Austrians took 300,000 prisoners, while another 300,000 soldiers disbanded and fled) provincial authorities lamented the peasants' negative feelings towards the war. In areas where both socialist and catholic unions were particularly strong, the landowners were worried by what they saw as signs of "red and white Leninism". Influenced by the peasant leagues' propaganda and surrounded by a peasant population that local authorities defined as anti-patriotic, many priests had from the start retained an attitude of indifference towards the military campaign, and resisted encouraging patriotism among the faithful. In July 1917, the socialist MP Claudio Treves uttered in parliament words that had a widespread echo among the masses: "next winter no longer in the trenches." (Treves 1917).

The following month, on 1 August 1917, pope Benedict XV sent an appeal to the heads of state of the combatant nations that sounded like a call for peace, asking them to end what increasingly appeared to be a "useless slaughter". The papal note found a very receptive audience, pronounced at a time of war weariness in all belligerent countries, reflected in the revolutionary insurrections in Russia, and in international peace meetings organised by socialists and by neutral countries. Although the pope had spoken of a "just peace" and not of peace at all costs, his message was isolated from the context in which it was made. He was accused by the interventionist front of supporting defeatism and weakening the internal front, especially in a situation where many catholics had responded patriotically, with chaplains at the front demonstrating how much liberal Italy needed the Church in order to maintain obedience in the army (Baldoli in Melloni 2020, p. 349).

From January 1918 the slogan "land to the peasantry" began to appear in both socialist and left-wing catholic newspapers, mixed with appreciation of the Russian events and the Bolshevik government. During the last year of the war in particular, issues of social change and pacifism were intertwined, although opposition to the war was repressed everywhere it appeared, and never threatened the Italian war effort. The activity of the trade unions and mass demonstrations for peace and bread in Turin in August 1917 exhibited a lack of interest in an Italian victory, revealing an unbridgeable gap between the Italian government and the masses in both the countryside and the factories. This was to become evident later, when in the 1919 elections a vast majority of votes went to the neutralist Italian Socialist Party (PSI) and the catholic Italian Popular Party (PPI) that had been founded in January 1919 by the priest Luigi Sturzo.

Throughout the war years, the socialist and neutralist press was hit by censorship and by a slanderous campaign from the patriotic and conservative press. Moreover, following the defeat at Caporetto, neutralist leaders found themselves physically attacked and taken to court by interventionists. Such trials almost invariably ended negatively for the neutralists and further encouraged their persecutors, who moved from verbal to physical assault, anticipating aspects of the fascist violence of the post-war years.

Imposed by the government on 24 May 1915 and supported by only a minority of the population, the war that resulted in 600,000 Italian dead, ended ultimately in victory for Italy. A group of about 200 nationalists, futurists, and interventionists from all sides met in the San Sepolcro square in the centre of Milan in March 1919, claiming the result of the war for themselves. This assembly, led by Mussolini, was the very foundation of the fascist movement, which called itself *fasci di combattimento*. These first *fasci*, despite their heterogeneity and confused programme (which included republicanism and votes for women, alongside nationalist aims), presented themselves as the heirs of the war, and soon showcased their anti-socialism by invading and destroying the headquarters of the PSI newspaper *Avanti!* [Forward!], also in Milan, in April.

Post-war Italy: from the "Red Biennial" to the "Black Biennial"

In the period following the defeat at Caporetto, three possible political solutions for the post-war settlement began to emerge. The first, heir to socialist neutralism and the ideals expressed at the international pacifist conferences at Zimmerwald and Kienthal (both in Switzerland, in September 1915 and April 1916 respectively), followed the Leninist direction to fight bourgeois governments and their war in order to create a revolutionary situation in which the working class would achieve power. Supporters of this course of action were the maximalist (revolutionary) current of the PSI, the workers' movement in industrial cities, and the peasants who occupied land during the so-called "red biennial" of 1919–1920.

A second proposal remained uncertain and vague: it was supported by interventionists of varied political origin, who claimed the rights of those who had prosecuted and won the war. Although after Caporetto democratic and nationalist interventionists appeared united in the defence of the nation from Austrian invasion, at the end of the conflict they began to divide among themselves, holding differing perspectives on the peace settlement. To illustrate the growing division, on 11 January 1919, a section of the nationalist movement protested during a public speech by Leonida Bissolati, the democratic interventionist and former leader of the PSI (who founded the Italian Socialist Reformist Party in 1912) at the Scala theatre in Milan, where Bissolati argued that Italy should renounce any aspirations towards Dalmatia in the name of the principles of national independence urged by US president Woodrow Wilson. The nationalists accused the Italian government of weakness during negotiations at Versailles, and the Allies of not rewarding Italy's victory. They claimed that Italy should be granted territory in Dalmatia and the port of Fiume (the latter not included in the secret Treaty of London between Italy and the Entente in 1915). At the Versailles peace conference, the other Allies agreed that Italy could complete its national unification by taking the Austrian territories in the north-east of the peninsula, but since Dalmatia only had a minority Italian population it was considered to be part of the new state of Yugoslavia. The acceptance of the terms of Versailles by prime minister Vittorio Emanuele Orlando was regarded by the nationalist right as a betrayal, what they called a "mutilated victory".

The third solution, an alternative to Bolshevism and ultranationalism, was represented by Bissolati's democratic interventionism: the democratic war would finally unite Italy, creating an enlarged state in which it would be possible to realise democratic reforms internally and a fraternal relationship with other countries externally. His speech in January 1919, although interrupted by nationalist heckling, supported the idea of a link between the country's security and democracy. Bissolati saw the annexation of Dalmatia as a mistaken ambition because it was a fundamentally Slav land; annexation would as a result attract nationalist hatred and future wars against Italy. Bissolati supported the idea that the war had been just, but rejected imperialistic claims for the post-war period. Unlike the nationalist press, which had unleashed aggressive anti-Bolshevik propaganda, Bissolati did not believe that a Bolshevik danger existed in Italy, as the socialist leaders had no real will to impose a communist society even if it was the desire of their numerous voters. Although Bissolati's attempt to support a Wilsonian programme still seemed possible in 1919, with the onset of the so-called "red biennial" that year, it became clear that the fight would be between the first two proposals, the nationalist and the "Bolshevik".

Influenced by events in Russia, the struggle of the peasant leagues and workers' trade unions promoted a pre-revolutionary climate. Social struggle broke out in the cities and the countryside, with popular revolts against the high cost of living. From June and July of 1919 there were strikes, trade union activity and urban protests, the looting of food shops, often with a high female participation, and popular insistence that food prices be halved. In the Po valley countryside, peasants went on strike and obtained wage increases and control of labour recruitment by the unions. The figures for trade union membership in the agricultural sector show an impressive growth from the pre-war period, with half a million members in 1919 and one million in 1920 for the socialist *Federterra* (National Federation of Agricultural Workers) and similar numbers for the catholic *Confederazione Italiana del Lavoro* (Italian Labour Federation, CIL) founded in September 1918. Even though the latter mainly organised sharecroppers and small landowners and acted with an anti-socialist purpose, it could not prevent the radicalisation of local catholic peasant leagues, which were committed to a high-level conflict particularly among wage-earning peasant labourers in parts of the Po valley (Crainz 1994, p. 158). By 1920 the PSI had some 200,000 members, while its associate trade union body, the *Confederazione Generale del Lavoro* (General Labour Federation, CGL), had grown from 250,000 in 1918 to 2,200,000 in 1920.

What really preoccupied the ruling class was not so much the number of trade union members, but the way they intended to call into question the existing relationship between social classes. In particular, landowners in the countryside interpreted peasant control of labour recruitment as an unprecedented intervention on the part of the unions, the sign of a radical change in labour relations. Not only did the unions change agrarian contracts, obtaining in many cases the 8-hour working day, but the left-wing parties managed to win elections at the local level. Although the Italian post-war period did not end in revolution, the struggle for land was part of a process that retained a revolutionary aspect by challenging property rights and the control of economic and productive resources (Bianchi 2006, p. 12; p. 31).

While the meeting at San Sepolcro, where the *fasci* were founded, went unnoticed in the press, the headlines from September 1919 were dominated by the occupation of Fiume, a town on the Dalmatian coast, by about 2500 soldiers led by the poet Gabriele D'Annunzio. He was a celebrity of the time and one of the most important voices of 1915 interventionism, and he chose to make Fiume the symbol of Italy's "mutilated victory". This was an open challenge to the government from the nationalist side, although it attracted people from all political backgrounds who were dissatisfied with the politics of liberal Italy. Fiume was only liberated, to be made a free city, by liberal prime minister Giolitti following the Rapallo conference in November 1920. The occupation of Fiume lasted 15 months, achieving significance as a nationalist focus and radicalising further those who took part.

Mussolini's *fasci* took part in the November 1919 national elections, but did not win a single seat in parliament, while the socialists obtained 156 seats and the catholic PPI 100, making them the two largest parties represented. Following the factory and land occupations of the summer-autumn of 1920, and the new PSI and PPI local election successes in October and November, the *fasci* organised in armed squads, unleashing violence against the socialists. Such violence was accompanied by the continual alarm raised in the bourgeois press about the Bolshevik danger, creating the idea that in some Italian regions social conflicts had undermined civil society, provoking attacks against property and the very existence of the wealthy classes, imposing a form of "plebeian tyranny" (Fincardi 2008, p. 86).

Despite the election successes and the demonstrations of force by the union movement, the socialists were deeply divided between a maximalist and a reformist current. At the national trade union (CGL) meeting on 11 September 1920, the reformist majority clarified that it did not consider the factory occupations as the first phase of the revolution. On 19 September an agreement with Giolitti's government conceded wage increases, while an accord was approved by the national steel workers' federation in Milan that led to the conclusion of the occupations. With the waning of the socialist trajectory and the inconclusive nature of the revolutionary impulse, the mobilisation of fascism began, largely financed by an agrarian and an industrial class that intended to withdraw any concession to the workers, and which was tolerated by a liberal ruling class worried by the socialist electoral gains at both national and local level.

What historian Emilio Gentile defined as an "anti-socialist civil war" (Gentile 2012 p. 20) spread violently from the Po valley to the rest of Italy, particularly to Tuscany, Umbria and Apulia. Fascist squad violence (*squadrismo*) increased during the political elections of May 1921, just when the *fasci* were included in Giolitti's national bloc in an attempt to "normalise" the radical threat they posed. While 35 fascist MPs entered parliament, fascist violence intensified, generally in connivance with the police, a situation that was further exacerbated by Giolitti's replacement by former socialist (and founder with Bissolati of the Italian Reformist Socialist Party in 1912) Ivanoe Bonomi as prime minister. A "pacification pact" with the socialists, encouraged by Bonomi and accepted by Mussolini, was rejected by the squad leaders, whose rebellion was, however, quelled by Mussolini's proposal to found a National Fascist Party (PNF) in 1921 that would retain a military organisation. The squads managed to impose themselves quickly as an armed faction in large parts of Italy, destroying in a few months the gains that the PSI had achieved over decades. At the local level, the struggle for power between 1920 and 1922 saw the fascists disputing, especially with the socialists, the right to run local institutions. From the autumn of 1920, following a substantial socialist victory at the local elections, the fascist squads began the practice of requesting and imposing on the government the resignation of local administrations, after having subjected them to violence, threats, and occupation—generally with no intervention from the police—making it impossible for them to function (Albanese in Isnenghi and Albanese 2008, pp. 318–319).

In 1921 this type of violence had spread so far that there were very few local administrations left that were hostile to fascism—a process that was completed by 1922, with the march on Rome in October as the final act. The relative ease with which the fascists conquered regions where the workers' presence was strong and rooted begs the question of what support they received from different social milieus. This was an issue not so much of the conquest of the state, but of the control of the periphery, where fascism asserted itself even before it was possible to predict or declare its final goal (Fincardi 2008, pp. 89–90).

The election results of 1921 confirmed the strength of the PPI, which increased its number of MPs from 100 in 1919 to 108, while the PSI's numbers decreased from 156 to 123, in part because of the communist defection in January (when the PSI revolutionaries abandoned the party to found the Communist Party of Italy). Delegates of the PPI entered the Bonomi government, which remained in office until February 1922, and then the two following governments led by liberal prime minister Luigi Facta (26 February-1 August 1922 and 1 August-31 October 1922).

In many Italian cities the fascists reacted against local socialist successes by organising punitive expeditions into the "red" zones, fire-raising and looting, all unpunished by the police and the many pro-fascist police commissioners. The violent leader of fascism in Cremona, Roberto Farinacci, later remembered: "Sure, the excesses of the fascists were many and very painful; and we can even accept as true the bleak amplification that was given by the leaders of the socialist party", even if the fascist reaction had been caused by the faults of the "Giolittian regime", responsible for the "Bolshevik turmoil" (Farinacci 1937, vol. 2, pp. 309–310).

During summer 1922, the fascists began to take control in local provinces and regions. These smaller "marches on the provinces" continued as fascist columns from all over Italy converged on the capital in late October. There were many references and symbols reminiscent of D'Annunzio's earlier march on Fiume, but the fascists also employed Giuseppe Garibaldi's slogan from the time of the struggle for the Italian unification in the nineteenth century: "Rome or death". About 50,000 people marched towards the capital, while thousands were simultaneously taking power in local centres all over Italy: they took control of city councils and the offices of the prefects, seized weapons, and destroyed the headquarters of the anti-fascist press. The march was organised by four men known as the *quadrumviri*: Cesare Maria De Vecchi, a landowner, and Emilio De Bono, a general, were monarchists; Michele Bianchi was a former revolutionary syndicalist; Italo Balbo was a former republican. These four symbolised the divergent origins of fascism, which interventionism had first brought together. While the *quadrumviri* were co-ordinating the columns marching towards the capital, Mussolini waited in Milan, uncertain whether the fascist march would succeed. Emilio Lussu, the veteran democratic interventionist and anti-fascist writer, observed in his account *The March on Rome and Thereabouts* that Mussolini stayed close enough to Switzerland so he could flee there if things went badly wrong further south (Lussu 1931).

Around 50 people (fascists, army officers, policemen, anti-fascists) were killed in the days leading up to the march on the capital; there was illegal activity, violence, destruction, and intimidation. It is difficult now to imagine a political movement in a modern democracy taking over the public sites of power across a country in just a few days. Although the police resisted occasionally, often they did not; and there was no longer any division within the movement – by this point Mussolini was its undisputed leader and king Victor Emmanuel III decided to entrust Mussolini with the role of prime minister.

With the new government, changes for the lower classes soon became evident. Shortly after the march on Rome, in the countryside, the new fascist organisations among the peasantry decided that landowners were entitled to recruit members from the fascist unions and reject those who belonged to the socialist or catholic unions. The new agrarian contracts in November 1922 were imposed by landowners and the fascist unions without consulting the socialist or catholic organisations. Fearful that the non-fascist unions might still be an effective force in some areas, prefects often arranged police control of public order. But for the peasants it was difficult to reject the new pacts and abstain from work because that would have meant losing their jobs. Indeed, those peasants who had been most involved in previous protests were dismissed. Workers could only join the fascist unions. Although the first agrarian contracts under Mussolini in 1922 retained the 8-hour working day and contained few novelties, in subsequent years contracts prohibited strike action, reduced wages, increased working hours, and cut the number of peasants employed; in short, they were a defeat for the peasant organisations.

The attitude of the Holy See was also crucial to the success of fascism. The papacy began to express an interest in fascism as early as 1922, considering it to be an interlocutor for a possible agreement between state and Church – an unresolved issue (the so-called Roman question) that had erupted following the Italian army's seizure of Rome, which became Italy's capital in 1870. At the beginning of October 1922, the Vatican's secretary of state, cardinal Pietro Gasparri sent a letter to Italian bishops asking all clergy to stay out of political disputes. By the end of the month, three days after the march on Rome, the new minister of education, Giovanni Gentile, had already announced his intended reform, which made the teaching of the catholic religion compulsory in all state primary schools, with decrees promulgated the following spring and autumn. While the Vatican daily *L'Osservatore Romano* and other newspapers close to the Holy See expressed open support for the fascist policies on education and religion, the PPI leader Sturzo remained opposed. He understood fully the ideological motives for the fascist reforms (Ceci 2013, p. 67).

However, it took some years before Mussolini was able to initiate his dictatorship, as he was still governing with a coalition (fascists, nationalists, liberals and conservative catholics) and with a parliamentary opposition. When the 1924 elections were conducted using violence and intimidation around the country, the socialist MP Giacomo Matteotti denounced the situation in the Chamber. His speech emphasised the greatest difference between fascism and its enemies: on the one side, the use of illegality and violence, on the other, the desire to re-establish legality and democracy. By then, almost all the socialist and democratic MPs had been physically attacked. In June 1924 Matteotti was kidnapped; liberal opponents asked the king to dismiss Mussolini, but he refused. The opposition abandoned parliament in protest and created an alternative parliament, called the Aventine secession after the name of the hill where, in ancient Roman times, the plebs gathered in protest against the patricians. In July, Mussolini declared: "It is not possible to step back now! Fascism did not achieve power through the normal ways. It did so with the march on Rome, an insurrectional act. If no one resisted, it was because it was clear that it was pointless to resist destiny". The significance of this speech was to confirm the legend of insurrection, but it also stated the truth about a ruling class that had not stopped fascism in 1922 and would not do so now. In August, Matteotti's corpse was discovered outside Rome. Unable to legislate, the Aventine secession was defeated; however, it was important from a moral point of view. Those who took the decision to leave the parliament erected an ethical barrier between the opposition and fascism, rejecting any compromise. Despite its defeat, this represented a strong moral message that could be passed on to the next anti-fascist generation.

The destruction of democratic institutions occurred in a short period between 1925 and 1927: laws against the freedom of the press and for the censorship of critical newspapers, the dissolution of political associations and any political party other than the PNF, a new penal code which transformed Italy legally into a totalitarian state, the reinstatement of the death penalty, the abolition of mayors and local city councils and their replacement by *podestà* (nominated by the government), the neutralisation of parliamentary powers so that only the Grand Council of Fascism (the supreme body of the Fascist party created in December 1922) remained, the institution of the Special Tribunal for State Security to deal with political opponents, and the establishment of the *confino* (internal confinement) to keep opponents for years, without trial, in remote villages in the south or on islands, all were put in place during those two years. These measures indicated a desire to return to values and priorities that challenged the Enlightenment heritage: authority came to be preferred to liberty and the rights of men and citizens were deemed to be outweighed by those of the *patria* (fatherland), which was in turn identified with the fascist state. As a result, many non-fascists had to pretend to be fascists, or risk being ostracised by the *patria* and losing their rights. In the late 1920s and particularly in the 1930s, it became impossible to work in the public sector without a party membership card (which for this reason began to be called the "bread card"). Fascism did not organise elections, but instead imposed directives from above; increasingly, as the dictatorship progressed, Mussolini became the central figure as the founder of the party, the head of the government, and *duce* (leader) of the Italian people—a Latin term (Dux) that did not mean anything in juridical terms but was supposed to indicate the existence of a mystical relationship of trust and communion between leader and led.

Contemporary Interpretations

The first attempts to explain the reasons for the emergence of fascism were advanced by contemporaries, mostly by those who had been defeated by the new movement. These first interpretations were characterised by the different political ideologies held by the intellectuals and political leaders involved, by their sense of responsibility for their own defeat, and by the new context in which they found themselves. This meant for many of them exile abroad, and was conditioned by the need to reorganise anti-fascist forces and to address a foreign audience.

During the interwar years, the nature of the debate on fascism was far from academic, as the historian Ernesto Ragionieri emphasised in a foreword to the communist leader Palmiro Togliatti's lectures on fascism, collected as a book in 1970, but delivered in Moscow in 1935 (Togliatti 1970, p. viii). Between 1924 and 1926 many anti-fascist intellectuals, political and trade union leaders who had avoided assassination or prison had fled abroad. Their analysis of fascism inevitably involved the practical aspects of political work and was based, as they saw it, on a struggle for their political existence. It also concerned a new political phenomenon whose temporal and spatial extension, origins and nature had evaded prediction.

Although the majority of the first works on fascism were published abroad, a clandestine press did exist in Italy in the 1920s, including a number of newspapers (albeit with an underground and precarious life) and small publishing houses. One of the latter was founded by a young democratic thinker and activist, Piero Gobetti, who published books by anti-fascists from different political backgrounds, including a volume entitled *Nazionalfascismo* in 1923 by the democratic liberal Luigi Salvatorelli. To study fascism in 1923 was to engage with a novel political phenomenon: was it revolutionary, as portrayed by its initiators and some of the autobiographies of those who took part in the foundation of the *fasci* at San Sepolcro? Or was it an armed movement in the hands of big capital and landownership?

The difficulty in understanding fascism contributed to a disorientation among all political and social forces, including the workers' movement, and as a result to an underestimation of the danger of fascism. The conservative right believed it would be able to control and absorb the movement after it had destroyed the workers' associations. And the left, from the anarchists to the communists, the socialists (both maximalist and reformist), and the peasant catholic trade unions, tended to consider fascism simply as an instrument of capitalist reaction. They did not see its capacity for autonomy, even from the sources that had financed it. But after the failure of the Aventine secession, and during the construction of the dictatorial regime, there was an attempt among anti-fascists to study more scrupulously the different components of fascism (Salvatorelli 1977, p. xiv; p. xx). Five classical explanations were developed regarding its origins: (1) the manifestation of a temporary aberration caused by the war; (2) an instrument of capitalism in crisis; (3) the mistakes of the left; (4) a revelation of profound characteristics in Italian society, as a result of the historical process through which Italy had been formed as a unitary and independent state; (5) the weaknesses of the liberal State. Other aspects that prompted investigation were the need to analyse fascism as an independent phenomenon, and the role of Mussolini. Moreover, the fascists too began to write about their own history. The first analyses of fascism developed at the same time as the struggle against it, and as a result were provisional and uncertain.

The First Coup: 1915

The first explanation was based on the circumstances of the First World War. For anti-fascists who had opposed the war, May 1915 was seen as the beginning of an authoritarian shift in Italian politics that continued to October 1922 and beyond. The declaration of war and the march on Rome were seen as two connected events, although the outcome was not regarded as inevitable, unlike the fascist interpretation of those events. When Salvatorelli's book was first published in 1923, he was a young correspondent on *La Stampa*, a newspaper based in Turin (but with national rather than local significance) and politically close to Giolitti. The newspaper had supported Giolitti's neutralism in 1915 and interpreted the so-called "radiant days" of May (when the interventionists demonstrated in Italian cities) as a coup by a minority which prevented the majority of parliament from freely expressing its will. The same forces that imposed their will in May 1915 were now, he argued, leading a movement against the liberal state (Salvatorelli 1977, p. xviii).

According to Filippo Turati, one of the founders of the PSI in 1892 and leader of its reformist current, the war ushered in a kind of dictatorship in every state involved, because the war effort subverted the functioning of the democratic order, enchained the liberal economy, familiarised young and old with the use of weapons, and exalted individual and collective homicide, blackmail, kidnapping, the torture of prisoners, punitive expeditions, summary execution, and every sort of crime with supposed national and patriotic aims. Writing from exile in 1928, he concluded that the war inculcated contempt for other people's lives, and even for one's own life and created the "jelly" in which the fascist virus could proliferate (Turati in Schiavi 1956, p. 123).

Antonio Gramsci, founder of the Communist Party of Italy in 1921, also argued that the germs of fascism were already present during the war, particularly during 1917–1918, when an authoritarian order that was typical of wartime measures resulted in the demolition of political opponents. In this dialectic relationship between fascism and state reaction Gramsci saw—both in the immediate post-war years and later in his prison notebooks—the continuity between pre-fascism and fascism. In January 1921 he wrote that the "complete decay" of the Italian parliament had begun during the war (Gramsci 1973, p. 98). Another founder of the communist party, Angelo Tasca, reflected in a book first published during his exile in Paris in 1938, that the carelessness with which part of the ruling class threw Italy into the war prepared the way for a disappointing peace settlement, which in turn contributed so much to the birth of fascism. During the struggle for intervention, interventionists of 1914–1915 began to deploy that complex of demagoguery, exasperated nationalism, and anti-socialism that was later found in the *fasci* of 1919–1922. The national war was conducted in an atmosphere of civil war: "between May 1915 and October 1922 the genesis is thus direct and uninterrupted" (Tasca 1965, p. 12).

Mussolini and the nationalists had everything to gain from portraying Italy as the "defeated" nation, even if it was far from the reality; probably no other country gained so much from the war, accomplishing national unity with the complete collapse of its historic enemy, the Habsburg empire. The ruling class, the nationalists, and the fascists who "mutilated" Italy's victory found that wounded national sentiment was the most effective means to fight for power and to wage war against the revolution of the "red biennial". Even anti-fascists who had been democratic interventionists during the war could see the poisoned seeds that it planted for the post-war period (Tasca 1965, p. 51). For example, Salvemini found himself next to Bissolati during the First World War, fighting in what he regarded as the last war for independence, conducted to ensure the dissolution of Austria-Hungary in the name of the fatherland and the oppressed nationalities. During the post-war period, opposed to any Italian intervention in Slav lands, Salvemini found himself in a difficult position, acknowledging the divisions within the interventionist front and the strengthening of those who had been neutralists. In his 1923 diary he depicted a profound and disillusioned re-evaluation of the intellectual position he had held in 1914–1918 (Franzinelli in Isnenghi and Ceschin 2008, pp. 378–382).

The fascists too insisted that the First World War had been crucial in creating a foundation for the regime. Victory against the external enemy in 1918 was followed by triumph against the internal enemy (ex-neutralist, socialist, Bolshevik) in 1922. For Volpe, a nationalist historian and fascist supporter, and member of parliament from 1924, the nation had moved during the war beyond the legal representation of an impotent parliament and had looked instead to the king and his government; the government became stronger as a result and imposed the nation on parliament. Some Italians already had a clear vision that one era of the nation's history had ended and another was beginning, both in domestic and international relations. In his view, fascism was a revolution—not Russian, but an Italian revolution, one that had begun in May

1915 and continued through the efforts of interventionists and combatants, and all those who fought the war with a spirit of voluntary enthusiasm (Volpe 1935, p. 13). The diaries and memoirs of fascists, many published for the celebrations of the "decennial" (ten years from the march on Rome) in 1932, all pointed to the roots of fascism in the First World War, as did the "Exhibition of the Fascist Revolution" in Rome in 1932. These diaries, although certainly updated for the decennial, had been written during the post-war years by squad leaders such as Farinacci, Balbo, Mario Piazzesi, and together with the many "histories of the fascist revolution", such as that by Giorgio Alberto Chiurco in 1929, depicted a clear, coherent and uninterrupted trajectory from 1914 until 1922. The violence committed by the *squadristi* was sanctified because it continued within Italy the revolution that the war had started. For example, a drama written by Farinacci in 1927 on the "fascist revolution" in Cremona was constructed around the character of a pacifist who came to understand his mistake after the war and turned to fascism, redeeming himself in part through violence that functioned in this case as an act of redemption (Farinacci 1927).

Fascism as the Armed Reaction of Capitalism

Between 1919 and 1921, the socialist newspaper *Avanti!* published a few cartoons representing fascism. They developed two main narratives: fascism was generally portrayed as a small *squadrista* dressed in black with a *fez* on his head, either held by a fat capitalist and shooting at the proletariat; or in the hands of an image of death—representing the war—placing him in a cradle as its child. In the last months of 1921, the anarchist and primary school teacher Luigi Fabbri wrote a short book, published in 1922, where he defined fascism as a "preventive counter-revolution": the war had radicalised the class struggle and the proletarian threat had disorientated the ruling class, of which fascism was "a sort of militia and a gathering centre" (Fabbri in De Felice 2005, p. 107). The fascists destroyed as many copies of his book as they could.

Gramsci agreed with this interpretation between 1921 and 1925, partly formalising it in the "Lyon Theses" of January 1926, during the third (clandestine) congress of the Italian communist party at Lyon, and more indirectly during the following years while he was in prison. As both a militant and a thinker, Gramsci maintained that the real fascism, the one that mattered, only began in 1920–1921 from a base in agrarian *squadrismo* and the capitalist bourgeoisie. However, he also recognised the important function of the petit bourgeoise, which gave fascism its own specific character. As early as May 1920, Gramsci forecast the danger of a reactionary coup. He was at that time involved in the movement of the factory councils in Turin and in production of the communist journal *L'Ordine Nuovo* [New Order] when he argued that the current phase of class struggle in Italy would be followed either by the conquest of power by the proletariat and a move to a new system of production and distribution, or by a terrible reaction on the side of the "propertied class and of the government caste". From 1921 Gramsci began to analyse the distinction between urban and rural fascism, starting with an article in *L'Ordine Nuovo* entitled "The two fascisms", on 25 August. Anticipating theories of fascist totalitarianism, he argued that fascism, as a new instrument of ruling class domination, aimed at realising an organic whole of all bourgeois forces in one political organism under the control of a single entity, which would direct the party, the government, and the state (Gramsci 1973, pp. 133–135). Having initially found its basis in the urban middle classes, fascism was becoming the form of organisation of the "most decisively reactionary section of the industrial and agrarian bourgeoisie" (Santarelli in Gramsci 1973, pp. 17–20). Gramsci insisted that the principal way of fighting fascism even after 1922 was an alliance with catholics on the left (for example, Guido Miglioli's peasant unions in the Po valley), democratic parties and groups of the petit bourgeoisie (for example, Lussu's *Partito Sardo d'Azione*—Sardinian Action Party), but all under the leadership of the communist party.

Like many thousands of communists from Italy and elsewhere, Togliatti (secretary of the party from 1927 following Gramsci's arrest) fled into exile, and finally settled in Moscow from 1934. In 1935, as a member of the Communist International (Comintern) secretariat, Togliatti held a course for the cadres of the Italian communist party in Moscow, in which much attention was devoted to the interpretation of fascism, a phenomenon he had studied since the 1920s, partly in debate with Gramsci. Togliatti began his analysis of fascism in October 1922, when he came to recognise the political, ideological and institutional novelty of fascism—in contrast to the predominantly economic interpretations that prevailed later in the Comintern. Starting with an analysis of the backwardness of Italian capitalism, he explained how the Italian workers' movement subverted the socialist party's effort to direct it. From socialist defeat came the success of fascism (Vacca 2022, p. 37). For Togliatti, fascism was the most powerful historical force ever developed for the preservation of a state as an expression of capitalist interests (Togliatti 1970, p. xiii). According to Joseph Stalin, fascism was a terrorist dictatorship of the most reactionary, chauvinist, and aggressive elements of finance capitalism, a definition picked up by the Bulgarian communist and general secretary of the Third International, Georgi Dimitrov, who ratified it at the seventh Congress of the International. This was the point of departure for Togliatti's lectures on fascism in 1935: however, in the Italian case, it was the agrarian owners who gave fascism its element of organisation, which industrialists later applied to urban areas (Togliatti 1970, p. 18).

At the 1926 communist party meeting at Lyon, fascism was described as a movement of armed reaction with the aim of disaggregating and disorganising the working classes; it could be understood within the traditional politics of the Italian ruling classes, and within the capitalist struggle against the working class. It was favoured in its origins by all the old ruling groups, but especially by the agrarians who found the pressure from the rural proletariat particularly threatening (*Tesi di Lione* in Bartolotti 1969, p. 101).

The (until 1929) communist Tasca also explored the relationship between early fascism and capitalism. He claimed that money paid by Italian industrialists allowed Mussolini to continue to maintain his "small army". Towards the end of 1919 the industrialists provided huge sums and Mussolini began a vast campaign on their behalf for naval and aerial armaments and the development of merchant shipping. In December, Mussolini proclaimed that he was beginning a fight for a foreign policy of expansionism (Tasca 1965, p. 58). The press of the socialists and left-wing catholics—victims of fascist violence in 1920–1922—emphasised the agrarian, rather than the fascist, involvement in violence against the peasants and trade unionists. The fascists were in that phase seen merely as an occasional, temporary instrument in the hands of landowners and industrialist.

Gramsci anticipated a 1930s debate that looked at fascism not simply as an Italian phenomenon. As a "capitalist reaction", with a mass basis in the small bourgeoisie, fascism was an international phenomenon that was more likely to succeed in backward countries, but could also spread all over Europe if the post-war economic crisis were not resolved (Vacca 2022, p. 43).

The Mistakes of the Italian Left

The second strand of argument to explain the fascist takeover focused not on the strengths of the fascist movement but on the failures of the Italian left. Gramsci began as early as 1923 to develop a fierce critique of the mistakes on the left that had allowed fascism to win: why had the parties of the proletariat been so weak from a revolutionary point of view? Why did they fail when they had to move from words to action? In 1924, particularly after Matteotti's kidnapping and murder, he focused his accusations on the non-communist opposition; this had also been a difficult confrontation between the two left-wing movements during the Aventine secession. In an article in the communist newspaper *L'Unità* [Unity] on 2 July 1924, Gramsci considered the Aventine opposition to be constitutional and impotent: the Aventine leaders were cultivating the illusion that the struggle against fascism could be resolved on a parliamentary level, forgetting that the fundamental nature of the fascist government was that of an armed dictatorship. A constitutional opposition could not prevent the illegal squad violence that operated directly in support of the capitalist-agrarian plutocracy. To defeat fascism, it was necessary to destroy those forces, and this could only be done through working class direct action; forces outside that class could support the struggle, but not lead it.

Gramsci was not the only one to consider the failure of the revolution, or of democracy more generally, in the immediate post-war years. During the interwar period, the different families of Italian socialism investigated the mistakes they had committed during the "red biennial". The maximalist leadership came under attack for its inconsistency in using revolutionary language while not seriously attempting any revolution, deluding the masses and leaving them without a clear direction.

Particularly hostile to the maximalist leadership was, understandably, the reformist leader Turati, who blamed the "Bolshevik myth" that spread everywhere as a messianic expectation of profound social renewal that could be universal and attained quickly. He deplored the demand for fantastic sudden wealth for workers, "just at the time when the needs of reconstruction imposed on everyone the most painful sacrifices", and condemned the illusion that the Russian phenomenon could take root in countries with very different conditions. The "hyperbolic" promises made during the war to the masses, despite the warnings of the moderate socialists, had been taken seriously and contributed in his view to the creation of the revolutionary myth. The occupation of the factories and its failure further weakened the socialist movement. When fascism was armed by reaction, the Bolshevik fever was already exhausting itself. Fascism arrived at the last minute to support the winners; winners out of a disorder that fascism itself had helped to create. The Bolshevik wave, despite its inconsistency, had offered fascism a pretext to present itself as the saviour. Without it, Turati claimed, the plutocratic-fascist conjunction would not have been possible (Turati in Schiavi 1956, pp. 122–130).

Even more critical of the socialist party was the ex-party leader, co-founder of the Italian Socialist Reformist party, and wartime interventionist, Bonomi, who was a minister under prime ministers Paolo Boselli (1916–1917), Orlando (1917–1919) and Giolitti (1920–1921), and prime minister between July 1921 and February 1922. Bonomi was political leader of the liberal state during crucial months in which fascism developed in strength, and fascist violence spread across the country. In a book published in 1924, Bonomi was particularly polemical against the socialist party for its political behaviour, and apologetic for liberal democracy, despite the responsibility of the liberal state, which he had represented, for bringing fascism to power. In his interpretation, it was possible as early as 1919 to feel, from the confused instinct of the masses, the terrible air of indiscipline, restlessness, and impatient aspiration for profound innovation that would later subject the Italian nation to a difficult test. The world seemed to be going left. Bolshevik Russia enlarged the hopes of the communists. The *fasci* participated in the atmosphere and, according to Bonomi, shared the same rhetoric. However, the first *fasci* failed; the proletariat grieved and suffered from the effects of the war and could not follow those who claimed to have supported it, preferring to look at the Bolshevik myth and its promise of social palingenesis. Workers' strikes multiplied and many city councils fell into socialist hands: the bourgeoisie seemed to surrender. It was at this point that the middle classes and industrialists turned to fascism—as an armed revenge against Bolshevism. It was, Bonomi argued, an insurrection of sections of the population against an intolerable situation. That was the moment when fascism, until then only a Milanese phenomenon, became national, attracting ex-servicemen, intellectuals, students, professionals, petit bourgeois, all moved by an idealistic spirit of liberty and patriotism against the brute violence of the uncultured masses (Bonomi 1924, pp. 218–227).

The socialist leader Pietro Nenni, ex-republican and democratic interventionist, also reflected, from exile in Paris, on the mistakes committed by both socialism and communism in confronting fascism. In Nenni's view, the congress of Livorno, at which the communist party was created in 1921, represented "the beginning of the tragedy of the Italian proletariat": "that secession, which left two communist parties in ferocious and ruthless struggle between themselves", was "the cause of the disorientation of the masses and offered them, unarmed, to the assaults of reaction". In his view, the Livorno congress seemed to ignore what was actually happening in the country. The violent attack of the communists against the old socialist party and the increasing divisions in the socialist movement between left and right factions led to the disintegration of working-class forces and, after the disillusionment of the "red biennial", to the diminished offensive and defensive capacity of those forces when it came to confronting the armed bourgeoisie. "The paths that were open to the socialists were therefore these: either an immediate revolutionary effort, or a clever parliamentary tactic, to open the way to a majority that could guarantee the proletariat the exercise of constitutional liberties and that could disarm the fascist squads" (Nenni 1976, pp. 137–148). In 1976 Nenni recalled his 1925 critique of both the maximalist and reformist currents of socialism and his support for a "revolutionary realism" that recognised that every class struggle was essentially a political struggle for power. He also recalled that he had attempted a campaign for the unity of socialism, begun in 1925 and completed in 1930 with the fusion of maximalists and reformists in Paris, but it came too late. The contradiction between reformism and intransigent maximalism had been, he concluded, a "torment" for the socialist movement (Nenni 1976, p. 20; p. 86).

The division that followed the congress of Livorno contributed to weakening the socialist party, although not significantly in electoral terms (the socialists obtained 123 seats and the communists only 15). A form of unity between socialists and communists, sought, for example, by Gramsci and Ruggero Grieco after 1924, was made impossible in 1921 by the conviction among communists that democracy was itself a form of dictatorship—the only difference was that by 1924 the fascist dictatorship was no longer masked. In this light, Togliatti argued in his 1935 lectures, the socialist strategy (followed particularly by reformists such as Turati or Treves) to counter fascism by involving all social classes was wrong: they elided the key leadership function that belonged to the proletariat in the fight against fascism (Togliatti 1935, p. 6). One aspect Togliatti thought was clear: it was impossible for the Italian ruling class any longer to apply the old politics, Giolittian and reformist, which had been based on concessions to particular social groups in order to maintain a form of "bourgeois parliamentary dictatorship". After the war, this way of doing politics no longer functioned because the working class and the peasantry rebelled. The PSI developed massively, with hundreds of thousands of members and millions of electors; and the peasantry developed extensive movements with the aim of occupying the land, which meant mass votes for the

PPI. At this point, the bourgeoisie decided to get rid of parliamentarism (Togliatti 1970, p. 16).

Few communists reflected more negatively on the left-wing failure than Tasca. He had been expelled from the communist party in 1929 because of his criticism of the Stalinist Third International theory of "social-fascism" that equated social democracy with fascism, and ended up in Paris where he published his views in 1938. Tasca blamed the lack of leadership for the would-be Italian revolution. In the Italy of 1919, the working class had been left without a programme and without leaders. The masses "continued to dream", but "their faith found no interpreters". In the meantime, the economic situation was becoming worse every month and strikes multiplied as the cost of living continued to rise. The government could not intervene everywhere, and the masses took to the streets all over the country, but there was no one to coordinate and direct such agitation. The maximalist direction of the PSI, argued Tasca, continued to postpone the revolution. After a failed internationalist strike in support of Bolshevik Russia in July 1919, the ruling class stopped worrying and could prepare for the fight (Tasca 1965, pp. 25–28). The *fasci*, "anaemic and almost non-existent" before September 1920, multiplied during the last three months of the year. It was not fascism that won the revolution, it was the inconsistency of the socialist revolution that provoked the emergence of fascism. With the factory occupations, the bourgeoisie was subjected to a psychological shock that explained its rage and determined its subsequent attitude. The industrialists felt that their rights of property and power were under attack, seeing themselves replaced in the factories, where work had continued in their absence. They showed bitterness and uncertainty, a strong rancour against Giolitti who "had not defended them" and resolved the situation by starting a fight to the death against the working class and the liberal state (Tasca 1965, pp. 129–130).

The catholic political movement also contributed to the socialist crisis because the PPI countered the socialist monopoly of the trade union movement, especially in the countryside—and Italy was still essentially a rural country. "If a Bolshevik danger ever existed in Italy", Tasca wrote, it was the PPI that averted it. Moreover, the party began to be subjected to strong right-wing pressure from the Vatican. In order to defeat the socialists, Mussolini needed help from the conservatives in the PPI, who became indispensable in the constitution of a coalition right-wing government. Mussolini believed he could achieve this with the help of the Vatican. When Benedict XV died and was replaced by Pius XI, Mussolini "rediscovered religion" and the universal mission of catholicism, as well as the important role of religion in pacifying the masses. In fact, this right wing had very little representation in the PPI, but could count on the support of the Vatican, while at the base, local catholic trade unions were in favour of an alliance with the socialists to defend trade union rights (Tasca 1965, p. 97).

Sturzo himself was not in favour of an alliance with the socialists, and the maximalists, too, made that impossible. Both parties at the national level deplored the accords their local representatives made in Cremona, the only city in Italy where PPI and socialist leaders agreed formally on a common strategy against fascism at the level of both municipal elections and trade union struggle in May 1922. Catholics who actively opposed fascism, such as Francesco Luigi Ferrari, Giuseppe Donati and Miglioli, interpreted Mussolini's movement as pagan and anti-Christian, as well as anti-democratic. They were led, as were many local priests, by their proximity to the lower classes, the peasants in particular. Some of them joined forces in 1922 around the newspaper *Il Domani d'Italia* [Italy's tomorrow], which sought to motivate the PPI to oppose fascism. For Miglioli, Giuseppe Speranzini and other leaders of the peasant catholic unions the socialist message was at heart a Christian message, and fascism represented its antithesis. However, while in parts of the Italian countryside fascist squad violence targeted priests, catholic leaders, and local PPI headquarters, in Rome, Mussolini began to devise an ecclesiastical policy that would bring him the support of the Vatican.

"Autobiography of the Nation": Fascism as a Revelation of Italian History

In 1922, Piero Gobetti, the 21-year-old precocious inspirer of liberal and radical anti-fascism, founded the newspaper *La Rivoluzione liberale* [Liberal revolution], after contributing to the cultural pages in Gramsci's *Ordine Nuovo*. Critical of a Risorgimento that had not inserted itself into the consciousness of the masses (a "failed revolution"), he believed that its mission now had to be renewed by a combination of critical intellectuals and the proletariat. Fascism embodied all the insufficiencies of the Italian nation and Gobetti opposed it with such strength and conviction that he was attacked both morally and physically by his fascist opponents. He fled to France in 1926, to die there as a result of the violence he had been subjected to.

The socialist Arturo Labriola, in *Storia di dieci anni. 1899–1909* [Ten years of history], a text that Gobetti would certainly have known, used the term "liberal revolution" to describe the full attainment of citizens' rights and to emphasise their absence in the history of a united Italy. To Gobetti, fascism's ascent to power replaced the political struggle against traditional paternalistic authoritarianism with the fundamental need to defend the most elementary rights of freedom. This new situation, which had been one of the possible outcomes of the Italian crisis, was evidence of the urgent need for a liberal revolution. Fascism was not an external agent, but had its roots firmly in the country's economic and social situation, and in its customs and habits. Fascism was an Italian phenomenon, a result of Italy's historical and economic immaturity, a resurgence of the Middle Ages (Alessandrone Perona in Gobetti 1995, pp. xxxiv–xxxvi).

Gobetti's interpretation of fascism—which particularly influenced the leaders of *Giustizia e Libertà* [Justice and Liberty], a democratic anti-fascist movement founded in Paris in 1929—was shared by a group of students and ex-combatants who gathered around Salvemini. They met in Florence in January 1925 to found a new weekly journal, *Non Mollare* [Do not give up], that was intended as a reproach and an exhortation to those who had begun to accept fascism as a given fact. At the beginning of the year, the journal's perspective was characterised by determination and optimism, with the fascists described simply as groups of violent cowards who were not worth taking seriously; however, by the autumn it had become almost impossible to keep publishing the journal because of continuous assaults and the arrest of contributors, and its editors had to admit that fascism had won. Fascism was at this point compared with an "army of occupation", against which it was technically impossible to revolt; it had at its disposal 200,000 blackshirts, all the military forces of the state, 100,000 carabinieri and the impunity "conceded to all the delinquents who were ready to act against the antifascists" (*Non Mollare*, n. 23, 5 October 1925). However, responsibility for fascism's criminal acts did not simply lie with Mussolini and the other fascist leaders, but was also shared by the Italian people. The former democratic interventionist and future *Giustizia e Libertà* militant Ernesto Rossi later deplored the passivity of Italians which arose "because of scarce moral vigour". It was, he concluded, a "serious symptom of the low level of our public morality" (Rossi 1945, p. 535).

If there was a time when hopes for a different outcome seemed realistic, it was a few years earlier during the "red biennial". Gobetti's need to understand the new social protagonists, and the dynamics within which they acted, led him to follow closely the reflections of *Ordine Nuovo*, by then oriented towards communism, and to see the emergence of a ruling elite among the working-class who had shown themselves able to lead and control the masses during the occupation of the factories in September 1920. A comparison with the Russian revolution, which Gobetti was also studying thoroughly, showed him the original character of this "Italian revolution" as radically innovative, not in terms of a new economic system but in its social and political structure. The major change was that now the people wanted power, and Gobetti interpreted this as a "new Risorgimento", Italy's first lay and democratic revolution (Alessandrone Perona in Gobetti 1995, pp. xli–xlii). Its defeat and the victory of fascism had averted that opportunity.

Gobetti's attitude to fascism was unequivocal: it was the expression of confused forces, outcast middle classes fearful of change, without any specific political culture, open to an authoritarian solution to social conflict. In November 1922 he wrote in *La Rivoluzione liberale* about the first Mussolini government, arguing that it was not just another conservative cabinet, but the "autobiography of the nation": "a nation that believes in class collaboration; that gives up on political struggle because of laziness". Fascism was also, he believed, a movement without ideology in which political adventurism was more important than theory. Fascism reduced ideas to a servile function, robbing them of dignity and autonomy. Above all, "Mussolinism" was most worrying because it confirmed the people's "courtier's habit" and "inadequate sense of responsibility". It was difficult to confront Mussolini because he had no coherence, no position, and was ready for any kind of transformism (Gobetti 1995, p. 176).

Gobetti's ideas were promoted, among others, by Carlo Rosselli, one of the principal organisers of anti-fascism amongst expatriates. He was captured after organising Turati's escape in November 1926 and sent to internal confinement on the island of Lipari, from where he escaped in 1929 with Lussu and Francesco Saverio Nitti. In France, Rosselli founded the movement *Giustizia e Libertà* that same year. Writing from exile, he shared Gobetti's argument that misery, indifference, and the centuries-long habit of renunciation meant that Italians lacked a sense of autonomy and responsibility. A servitude that had lasted for centuries ensured that the average Italian was still caught between the resignation of the slave and the urge for anarchist revolt. Rosselli regretted that Italians had no conception of life as a struggle and a mission, of the notion of freedom as a moral duty, no awareness of the limits of their own and other people's rights. Catholic education and a series of patronising governments had prevented Italians from thinking critically for centuries. Poverty had completed the picture. Even in the twentieth century, Rosselli thought, the average Italian relinquished their spiritual independence to the Church. The intervention of a leader—whether the Pope, the king or Mussolini—often satisfied their psychological needs (Rosselli 1945, pp. 109–110).

Despite appearances, fascism was for Rosselli the most passive result of Italian history, a gigantic return to past centuries, an abject phenomenon of adaptation and renunciation. Even the struggle for independence had been the work of minorities and not the passion of a people. Only a few northern urban centres had actively participated in the revolt against Habsburg rule. Following victory over the Austrians, the Savoy monarchy quickly replaced the existing rulers in the centre and south. The Piedmontese bureaucracy trapped the whole of Italy, paralysing the last attempts at autonomy. The triumph of the monarchist and diplomatic current managed, as in Germany, to separate the myth of unification from the ideal of liberty. Democratic republicans such as Mazzini and Carlo Cattaneo were the vanquished of the Risorgimento (Rosselli 1945, p. 111).

Gramsci too, in his reflections on the regime during his years in prison, collected and published as *Prison Notebooks* in 1948, argued that the democratic leaders of the Risorgimento had failed to mobilise support beyond sections of the small bourgeoisie and of the urban proletariat, crucially neglecting the peasant masses and, in the process, a transformation of agriculture. Mazzini and the democrats were unable to pursue a Jacobin policy as France had done after the revolution, with radical agrarian reform and the rejection of any compromise with the conservative forces of the bourgeoisie. The moderates' victory during the final phase of the Risorgimento resulted in the formation of an independent state that lacked effective "popular-national" unity. The gap was maintained between ruling class and popular masses, and the ruling class remained permeated by a conservatism that degenerated into "reactionism" in moments of crisis. The culture of the intellectuals did not reach the people, and the social-economic imbalance between more and less advanced geographical areas worsened (contributing to the so-called "Southern question", a richer north and a poorer south). The choices made by the Italian bourgeoisie after the Risorgimento had an impact on Italy's subsequent development, leaving the task of realising national-popular unity to the working class through an alliance of the exploited classes, and crucially with the peasantry (Gramsci 1959, pp. 15–16).

Tasca, like Gramsci and Rosselli, also speculated about the possible historical causes of fascism. After 1870 the old oligarchies had one preoccupation: to prevent the ascent of the third estate or delay it for as long as possible, blocking every avenue that could have led to working-class action and political consciousness. Two conflicting forces came together to avert danger from below: the monarchy and the Vatican. The integration of the working class into the state progressed, but was interrupted by the war. Fascism had to an extent been the autobiography of a nation that had given up on political struggle, had the cult of unanimity, "shied away from heresy". Fighting fascism did not, therefore, mean only fighting a ferocious and blind class reaction, but also a certain mentality, a sensibility rooted among a large section of the population (Tasca 1965, p. 537; p. 135).

The political immaturity of Italians was an argument that the anarchist Camillo Berneri (former student of Salvemini and a prominent member of the exile Italian community in Paris, killed in Barcelona during the Spanish Civil War by Stalinists) also made, in a book first published in Spain in 1934. According to Berneri, if an adventurer like Mussolini could achieve power it showed that the country was neither politically healthy nor mature. Italians had to get rid not only of Mussolini but also of the defects that had enabled the victory of fascism. Berneri argued that even heroes, acting alone against the dictator, like the two anarchists Michele Schirru or Gino Lucetti, sentenced, respectively, to death and 30 years imprisonment by the Special Tribunal for plots and attempts on Mussolini's life, were in fact an expression of a depressed country. The whole of the Risorgimento had been full of individual actions, of crazy displays of heroism, but also of many and prolonged acts of cowardice: "We have always had dictators, ministerial demiurges, great agitators, and manipulators of parliamentary majorities. Individuality has always been the dominant characteristic of Italian public life" (Berneri 2007, p. 86).

In these early interpretations, it is apparent that fascism was seen as a typically Italian phenomenon rooted in its recent history. According to Nenni, for example, it was not the case that fascism was a pure fact of bourgeois reaction. Fascism was "incomprehensible without taking into account the history and the social and moral character of our country, and with profound roots in the popular and plebeian element". This last aspect should have mostly worried the socialist leaders, as it illuminated the gap between the party and the country (Nenni 1976, p. 179). Further reflections were advanced by the writer Ignazio Silone, the pseudonym of Secondino Tranquilli who, in 1926, at the time of the fascist laws, was a 26-year-old leader of the communist party who escaped prison and fled abroad, leading the illegal centre of the party for three years. He went to Moscow, Basel and Berlin and finally settled in Switzerland, where in 1930 he proclaimed his disagreement with the party line on "social-fascism". He dedicated himself to writing and became successful as Ignazio Silone with his novel *Fontamara*, which revealed the harsh conditions of life in the Abruzzo countryside under fascism. In 1941 he revived his political commitment and created the new centre of the PSI in Zurich.

The works on fascism written abroad by exiles were characterised by the political and existential context in which they lived. The analyses of Silone and of Tasca were influenced by their militancy, and by their subsequent conflict and break with the communist party. Silone's work on fascism drew a negative judgment of the Italian situation in the decades after unification, characterised (in contrast with other European countries, he believed) by economic backwardness, political imbalances, the southern question, and the Roman question. The coming of dictatorship could be understood in terms of historic symptoms such as the persistent hegemony of a moderate political leadership, the immaturity of innovative forces, scant popular involvement in the movement for unification, and the absence of strong democratic state traditions (Silone 2002, pp. 3–11).

The Crisis of the Liberal State

Not all anti-fascists pointed to the faults of the liberal state and the Risorgimento process. Liberal politicians and intellectuals, on the contrary, portrayed the process that began with the Piedmontese statesman Camillo Benso Count of Cavour in the 1850s as one of democracy, liberal political freedom, and internationalist diplomacy, and regarded fascism as an interruption in an age of progress. The liberal philosopher Benedetto Croce, although he recognised the weakness of the governments that permitted the two coups of 1915 and 1922, was convinced that fascism was a 20 year-long parenthesis that should not be overemphasised when considering the previous centuries of glorious Italian history, which were taken to their highest level by the Risorgimento and the subsequent period of economic, cultural and political progress (Croce 1944, pp. 13–18).

In one of his many anti-fascist articles written in 1923 in the liberal newspaper *Il Mondo* [The World], the journalist, philosopher and liberal democratic politician Giovanni Amendola (who died in exile in France in 1926 as a result of three fascist assaults) specifically defended Cavour as the guarantor of parliamentary independence. The Piedmontese statesman had been able to protect the constitution against attacks by both the extreme left and right, successfully creating and sustaining a moderate majority—the same constitution that was now denigrated by Mussolini's government. Nevertheless, Amendola did not glorify Italian liberalism as it developed after Cavour, but lamented the lack of successors in the liberal moderate tradition (Amendola 1960, pp. 129–130). In

1924, he pointed at Antonio Salandra (prime minister in 1914–1916 and liberal supporter of Mussolini's government in 1922) as an example of the crisis of the liberal state: by supporting Mussolini's government, the former prime minister moved away from the historical intellectual tradition of Italian liberalism, which would never have accepted any regime based on violence rather than consensus. On the contrary, the historical right in the nineteenth century, building on Cavour's democratic system of alliances, had supported the need for political freedoms (Amendola 1960, p. 272). In 1925 Amendola described fascism as interrupting that tradition and moving towards what he had already described as a totalitarian system, which tolerated only the citizens who adhered to fascism, excluding anti-fascists from public life, denying even their right to exist (Amendola 1960, p. 85).

Accusations against the liberal system for allowing the fascist seizure of power was more evident from the socialists. As Nenni well remembered, by 1921 in the whole of Italy the "terroristic and illegal organisation of the capitalist bourgeoisie completely replaced the constitutional state, its laws and its institutions". Everywhere the forces of the state (police, army, judicial system) submitted themselves to the fascists, who were certain "not only of impunity, but of their support" (Nenni 1976, p. 141). Despite this, the socialists obtained a huge election victory in May 1921. Fascism was well-organised by the end of 1921, but had it not enjoyed the support of the liberal state, had it been compelled to fight using only its own strength, the proletariat would have been able to confront it. The disproportion arose from the fact that the proletariat was disarmed and fascism was armed; the proletariat was threatened with prison and starvation, while the fascists acted in plain sight of the authorities. This truth did not imply that the fascists did not have their own dead: they had to face individual retaliation, but the socialist proletariat was never in a position to organise its own resistance or an offensive using military means (Nenni 1976, p. 181).

One of the most detailed discussions on the crisis of the state that opened the way to fascism was made once again by Tasca. In his view, it was principally the government of Nitti (prime minister from June 1919 to June 1920, in exile from 1924) that had made a coalition with the socialists impossible. The socialists would not collaborate with Nitti, a liberal who underestimated fascism, and was responsible for the reorganisation of the police forces in 1919, including the so-called "regal guard", which was employed actively in the repression of popular demonstrations. Between October 1919 and May 1920 several hundred workers and peasants were killed in Italy by the police. Nitti's other possible allies could have included the members of the PPI, neutralists in their majority (an attitude that gave them great success in the elections of 1919 and 1921), but they in turn considered Nitti to be too compromised by participation in wartime government. At the same time, the right-wing opposition focused all its efforts in taking down Nitti and his foreign policy. The socialists also continued to remain outside Giolitti government that followed Nitti: when Giolitti proposed that socialists should enter the government, Turati refused because he knew the party would not follow him. The worsening economic crisis made traditional attempts at negotiation even more difficult. Like Nenni, Tasca pointed also to the liberal state's collusion with fascism, arguing that local functionaries often sympathised with the *fasci* or with their powerful protectors. The military character of the fascist reaction ensured unquestionable superiority: it took the struggle to a level for which the socialist opposition had not prepared (Tasca 1965, pp. 100–120; pp. 187–188).

Autobiography of Fascism

Fascist writers, for obvious reasons, analysed the years of war and post-war crisis from a very different standpoint. Volpe, writing in 1935, described his view of the purpose of fascism and the intellectual influences that had shaped it. At the root of fascism was a form of syndicalism, influenced by the French philosophers Henri Bergson and Georges Sorel, in which the proletariat was trusted together with the bourgeoisie to create new conditions for working-class society, and which did not exclude colonialism or war, both of which were said to possess creative virtue. Volpe, a former nationalist, stressed the importance of nationalist leader Enrico Corradini's movement (the Italian Nationalist Association, founded in 1910), which opposed the egalitarianism of political democracy, affirmed the nation and its individuality against socialist or clerical internationalism, and which called for a colonial policy, together with a policy towards emigration to ensure that it did not constitute an impoverishment of the nation. This nationalism represented the values of the productive bourgeoisie, but also considered the idea of creating workers' unions that would collaborate with the nation rather than oppose it. It supported a form of social solidarity between classes with the aim of enhancing national power (Volpe 1935, p. 20).

As we have seen, the point of departure of the fascist narrative was the First World War—as exemplified in the "Exhibition of the Fascist Revolution" that opened in Rome in 1932, where the first march in 1915 was aligned with the second in 1922, an external war that continued after 1918 against the internal enemy, the two steps of the "revolution". Volpe himself, as a history professor, was called on during the First World War to support soldiers' morale. For him, the war was the final stage of the Risorgimento, which had been the work of political minorities and calculated diplomacy; the war would finally reveal the authentic character of the new Italian. Volpe's conversion to fascism, however, belonged to the post-war period, during the "red biennial" and the question of the "mutilated" victory in which Italy was regarded as a defeated ally, despite being one of the winners. It was fascism that emerged as a force for national renewal. In 1924, elected to the parliament on the fascist list, Volpe wrote that fascism was the expression of "the whole of Italian life in the last twenty or thirty years". Influenced by his Medieval and Early Modern studies, in 1925 he drew a parallel between the revolution of the Renaissance, which was accomplished by intellectuals, and the current revolution, which saw the participation of "the people", namely of "all the forces organically melted together that formed a nation" (Giarrizzo in Bonuglia 2007, pp. 27–37). One positive result of the First World War was that it had emphasised the crisis of socialism and of liberalism: the "internal Caporetto" (the "red biennial") resulted in fascist resistance, just as in 1917 and 1918. Violence was a necessity in this act of national redemption, a violence that Volpe defined as "chivalric and romantic", "disciplined", "honest and loyal" (Aliberti in Bonuglia 2007, pp. 62–64).

Volpe's interpretation of the war and fascism as a continuation of the Risorgimento drew on the theories of the philosopher Giovanni Gentile. A convinced interventionist, Gentile interpreted the European conflict as the coronation of the wars for Italy's independence. His collaboration with Mussolini began during the war, and they shared the perception of the post-war period as a continuation of the struggle against the internal enemy—the socialists and catholics who had opposed the war. In his view, the Risorgimento lived on in the fascist regime, as yet incomplete and still in the making. Fascism was thus inserted into the long-term history of Italy, so that the fascist black-shirts could be seen as a continuation of the Garibaldi "red shirts" of the nineteenth century. Both Gentile and Volpe rejected the interpretation of fascism as a parenthesis, a superficial phenomenon linked to the contingencies of the post-war struggle against socialism (Franzinelli 2021, pp. 10–23). Another fascist intellectual, Giuseppe Bottai, recognised the war as the first step in his fascist itinerary, to the extent that he felt his own adult life had only begun when he volunteered for the front, as someone profoundly disillusioned by the parliamentary system and anxious to rebuild the nation, like many interventionists. In the post-war years, Bottai found it natural to take part in nationalist demonstrations for Italian rights in Dalmatia. Arrested following violent clashes, he became a prominent figure, acquiring some notoriety under the Nitti government. He too was influenced by Gentile's interpretation of fascism as a continuation of the Risorgimento, establishing a link between the regime and an earlier Italian national tradition (Galfré 2000, pp. 12–20).

A majority of fascist leaders, uninterested in such philosophical and historical interpretations, simply glorified violence and the conquest of power as an anti-socialist revolution. Farinacci published books that reflected this outlook, while condemning the liberal ruling class for the failure to accomplish more for Italy from victory in the First World War. It was the war, he claimed, that led the Italian people to acquire a political consciousness of unity. Isolated by the neutralist masses in 1914, the interventionists and, later, the combatants felt even more betrayed during the post-war years, which Farinacci depicted as a period of "Bolshevism", from which they were rescued and vindicated by the eventual triumph of fascism (Farinacci 1937, vol. 1, chapter 1). Similar views were held by the nationalist journalist (and later fascist diplomat) Attilio Tamaro, who argued that Italy represented a proletarian country that, having contributed to victory, now risked being repudiated by the Allied nations that no longer needed its help (Tamaro 1953, pp. 51–52). The spirit of rancour and disillusionment directed at liberal Italy was also commonly found in the diaries and histories of fascism written by, among others, Chiurco, Balbo and Piazzesi. They interpreted the post-war years as if there were two Italies separated by an immeasurable gap. Confronting what they saw as a time of pro-Russian enthusiasm among the masses, they all proclaimed that fascism and the necessary violence that accompanied it had saved the nation. According to Balbo there was no possible compromise between "us" and "the opponents": the war had "cut Italy's history in two" and had changed the spirit and the language of politics, which explained the ferocity directed against the internal enemy, who was hated even more than the external foe (Balbo 1932, p. 29).

An "Anti-Party"?

Most of the contemporary interpretations of fascism tended to describe it as if it was a unitary phenomenon: a parenthesis in Italian history, a revelation of Italian history, a dictatorship of finance capital, a petit-bourgeois reaction, and so on. As historian Renzo De Felice commented in his foreword to Tasca's book, each of these had aspects of validity, but there existed in different chronological phases several types of fascism, some of them more evident and triumphant, some more hidden or repressed, and, as we shall see, recent historiography has shown how fascism was indeed comprised of multiple and sometimes contradictory tendencies. The most complicated question at the time of the regime itself was defining fascism in its own terms, rather than identifying it as the result of external factors (De Felice in Tasca 1965, pp. xii).

In 1923 Salvatorelli was one of the first to describe the main character of fascism as the "revolt" of the middle classes. The petit bourgeoisie felt strangled between big capital and the working class and wanted to defend its autonomy. He saw two distinct elements in fascism that expressed themselves almost simultaneously from the very start: first the progressive San Sepolcro social programme of 23 March 1919, which included a republican stance and supported female suffrage, and secondly the anti-socialist actions, when the fascists assaulted and devastated the headquarters of the national newspaper of the PSI, *Avanti!*, on 15 April (Salvatorelli 1977, p. xvi). The anti-socialist aspect was the most evident as the movement developed, which enabled it to pose as a preventive reaction to an alleged proletarian revolution, which won for it both the capitalists' money and the state's tolerance. The nationalist rhetoric that was present from the time of the First World War and was confirmed at San Sepolcro led the movement to see the proletariat as the denier of patriotism.

The left built on this view of fascist origins. Tasca reached similar conclusions to Gramsci (spelt out in the Lyon Theses) in arguing that fascism was not solely a weapon of the bourgeoisie, but also a social movement with its own characteristics, while, for communist leader Amadeo Bordiga, fascism won mainly as a result right-wing reaction to the politics of concessions to the workers by the left-wing bourgeoisie during the democratic period. Tasca also paid special attention to the ex-combatants, who were, in their majority, Wilsonian and democratic, with a generic but sincere desire for social renewal, but diffident towards the old ruling class (Tasca 1965, p. 19). Togliatti, too, reflected that these former combatants, who felt outcast in the post-war years, were not isolated individuals but a mass, and represented a phenomenon that had class aspects. The communists, Togliatti later claimed, had not understood that the veterans could not simply be ignored. Their duty had been to win over enough of them to avoid the ex-combatants being manipulated by the bourgeoisie: this task was not accomplished and that had been a mistake. Such a failure meant that the intermediate social strata moved towards the bourgeoisie, who did indeed exploit them as a source of support (Togliatti 1970, pp. 9–17).

At first fascism was not homogeneous. For example, Nenni, like others who would later be anti-fascists, took part in the meeting at San Sepolcro, where different elements came together, but did not march side-by-side thereafter. San Sepolcro reflected the reality of urban fascism, but rural fascism emerged later, in 1920, in the shape of squads armed for the fight against the rural proletariat; *squadrismo* gathered social outcasts, petit bourgeois, and intermediate social strata against a common enemy, the working class.

Tasca was one of the first to point to the fact that, from the very start, Mussolini needed money and could only look to the industrialists and the agrarian landowners to find it. He succeeded in finding a way to address both the confused passions of the masses and the precise interests of the capitalists. This bivalence was fundamental to understanding early fascism. Reading the San Sepolcro programme, fascism was, at that point, more to the left than Mussolini would have liked, although it also contained a section on foreign policy that, while professing to disapprove of any imperialism, supported Italy's rights in the Adriatic and implicitly the theory of Italy's "mutilated" victory. The fascists, Tasca argued, were neither republican nor monarchist, neither catholic nor anti-catholic, neither socialist nor anti-socialist; they supported class collaboration or class struggle, depending on the opportunity; since a political party required a programme and a doctrine, they were an anti-party. Mussolini himself said that they had no doctrine: "our doctrine is fact" (Tasca pp. 52–56).

Gramsci reached the same conclusion in an article in *Ordine Nuovo* in 1921, when he stated that fascism could only be partially seen as a class phenomenon; fascism "presented itself as the anti-party, opening the doors to any candidate, allowing, with its promise of impunity, a generic multitude to cover, with a veneer of vague and nebulous political ideals, the wild outburst of passions, hatreds and desires". In this way it had come to identify itself with the barbaric and antisocial psychology of a certain strata of the Italian people (a "semi-barbarian terrain"), who had not yet been changed by new traditions, by schooling, by the experience of living together in a well-administered state (Gramsci 2019, p. 64).

The reformist socialist Giovanni Zibordi noted as early as 1922 that fascism was not a new party, but was at the margins of various bourgeois parties, and received from all of them a contribution "of forces or of membership", that served all of them "as an outlet". It was the expression, the interpreter, and the instrument of a counter-revolution against a proletarian revolution that did not happen, either as a threat or a programme. Fascism nevertheless got lost in the large urban centres, which it could not dominate for strategic and tactical reasons because of the numeric power of the working classes, and the presence of more vigilant, energetic, and independent local authorities. In these towns and cities, fascism took a more political, national, intellectual, and literary character and did not engage in economic or military action (Zibordi in De Felice 2005, pp. 254–255).

It was also difficult to define precisely what fascist ideology was. Togliatti thought that it was an eclectic ideology, in which a constant was the nationalist element—even more so in Germany because of defeat in the war. Alongside this element were other aspects: corporatism, for example, the basis of which was class collaboration, was not invented by fascism but by social democracy (Togliatti, p. 14). With the constitution of the party in 1921, new programmatic lines erased the 1919 programme, but this had no impact on the support for fascism: the fascist "mass", Tasca believed, had no interest in any ideology (Tasca 1965, p. 155).

It took some time before anti-fascists began to think of fascism as not solely an Italian phenomenon. According to Tasca, it was also chronologically limited: a fact of the post-war period, fascism could not be compared with Bonapartism or anything that had happened before (Tasca 1965, p. 554). Nevertheless, the networks of exiles and militants who met in several European cities at international congresses on peace and human rights in the interwar years began to discuss fascism as a danger for the whole of Europe, and a phenomenon that could be exported, particularly from the late 1920s and the economic crisis. The growth of fascism in Austria and Germany in particular, and the links it seemed to be establishing with industrial elites, suggested that fascism was no longer specifically Italian and that its threat to other countries became a very urgent matter.

Making Sense of Mussolini

It was particularly difficult for anti-fascists to find the necessary detachment to analyse Mussolini's role in the success of fascism. After all, for the socialists, he had been a comrade until 1914, so it was inevitable to feel strong emotions towards someone who now appeared as a traitor. The result was a tendency to underestimate Mussolini intellectually and to downplay his importance; to depict him as an opportunist and an adventurer who could only achieve success thanks to the support of capitalism, or because of the long-term weaknesses of Italian democracy.

In reflections published in Spain in 1934, the anarchist Berneri tended to diminish Mussolini's ideology. The *duce* was a man who had at heart only one real wish: to maintain power for as long as possible and to continue to strengthen it. Berneri nonetheless looked for a deeper reason for Mussolini's success: his charisma. He admitted that Mussolini was an effective orator and remembered his speeches as a revolutionary socialist leader: "I can still see his visionary eyes, the arms stretched out in front of him and shaken by an unrestrained tremor, his hammering utterances. And I think, with melancholia, about the idolatry he enjoyed among the young" (Berneri 2007, pp. 20–21; p. 54). Berneri was not linked to any political party so felt freer to analyse links between the left parties and the origins of fascism. He criticised the fetishist attachment of the masses to leaders such as the revolutionary syndicalist Alceste De Ambris and the left-wing catholic Miglioli, who were "worshipped irrationally". Berneri also underlined that many supporters of Mussolini, among the *ras* (local fascist leaders) and the hierarchies of fascism, were of "subversive origin", people who had changed flag; this was a very sensitive argument for the left.

Gramsci, in the fourth volume of his prison notebooks, reflected on the fact that, at a certain point in historical development, social classes began to detach themselves from traditional political parties: this was "the most delicate and dangerous phase" because it left the field open to charismatic men who appeared "sent from Providence"—as the Pope said of Mussolini in 1926 (Gramsci 2019, p. 103). Croce in 1944 reflected on the figure of the *duce* as superman, which derived from the model of D'Annunzio. It was an idea found among ex-combatants who could not adapt back to civil life (Croce 1944, pp. 55–56). In fact, Mussolini's trampoline had been socialism: within a few years he had moved to the highest role in the party, as director of its newspaper *Avanti!* (1912–1914). Before him, Enrico Ferri, also director of the newspaper (1903–1908), had been immensely popular among the masses. According to Gramsci, the need for a leader corresponded to a primitive phase of the socialist parties: the heroic and individual conception of political struggle that belonged to the democratic and Garibaldian tradition, while a more mature socialism would emancipate itself from the cult of the charismatic leader. However, in reality socialist education was still largely reliant on the sentimental link between the leader and the masses, and counted on the emotional identification that the latter felt with their leaders. The proletariat venerated unconditionally, with an almost religious respect, the symbols of its organisation and the leaders' images. Reliant on their personalities and capacity to spark the admiration of the crowds, leaders communicated through symbolic meanings, rather than through concrete political actions; this resulted in an image of the leader's superiority compared with other people, not only as a political guide, but as a human being (*Memoria e Ricerca* 2021).

This was also true of Mussolini, not only as a socialist leader, but also during the First World War, when he constructed his own myth as a "*duce* in the making" through his articles and correspondence from the front in his interventionist newspaper *Il Popolo d'Italia* (Mussolini 2016). Tasca noted that Mussolini did not take part in serious actions during the war because his life was "too precious", but his 38 days in the trenches were enough to legitimise him and his newspaper (Tasca, p. 43).

Instead, Silone downplayed Mussolini's role. He interpreted the "red biennial" as the moment of irreversible crisis of the liberal system. Parts of his book repeat arguments of the Third International, with its complete rejection of reformist socialism, which was blamed as the main cause of the defeat of the workers' movement. Fascism was presented as the inevitable winner, having the support of the bourgeois parties—reformists, conservative catholics, liberals, and democrats—so that Mussolini appears as less important and perhaps even replaceable. He was an anti-revolutionary who used revolutionary methods, a clever strategist—but also, as for other exiles, a traitor (Franzinelli in Silone 2002).

One of the first anti-fascist biographies of Mussolini was written between 1938 and 1942 by the democratic liberal journalist from Avellino, Guido Dorso, who collaborated with Gobetti and later adhered to *Giustizia e libertà*. He collected a vast number of documents on Mussolini's political evolution from the First World War to the march on Rome, and contributed to an analysis of Mussolini's rise to power which he framed in the context of Italian interventionism, post-war economic crisis, the defeat of the socialist revolution and the support that sections of the state provided to the fascist squads and the fascist party. Dorso underlined some continuities in Mussolini's trajectory from the time of interventionism onwards: his (at first only verbal) violence, anti-parliamentarism, and hatred for the socialist party (Dorso 1949, pp. 145; 179). He provided a first critical study of Mussolini's speeches, emphasising throughout how they were fragmentary, inconclusive, and contradictory. Mussolini's participation in the 1921 elections in Giolitti's national blocs were simply part of a two-faced game that he could play from parliament, after founding a party that did not have a precise programme. It was indeed his "relativism" that allowed him to have "no faith, no ideas, no programmes", to "renew himself every morning without fear of contradicting himself" (Dorso 1949, p. 245; p. 283).

Dorso's book was published two years after his death, in 1949, when historians began, in the new democratic climate of a republic based on a new anti-fascist constitution (from 1948) and on the unity of anti-fascist parties, to attempt a new study of the previous twenty years. This had to begin by focusing not only on the origins of fascism, as much of the interwar literature had done, but also on the regime that fascism had operated from 1922 to the final collapse of the fascist project in 1945.

References

Amendola, Giovanni, *La democrazia italiana contro il fascismo, 1922–1924* (Milan and Naples: Ricciardi, 1960).
Balbo, Italo, *Diario 1922* (Milan: Mondadori, 1932).
Berneri, Camillo, *Mussolini grande attore. Scritti su razzismo, dittatura e psicologia delle masse*, ed. by Alberto Cavaglion (Santa Maria Capua Vetere: Spartaco, 2007; 1st ed., Spain 1934).

Bianchi, Roberto, *Pace, pane, terra. Il 1919 in Italia* (Rome: Odradek, 2006).
Bonomi, Ivanoe, *Dal socialismo al fascismo* (Rome: Formiggini, 1924).
Giarrizzo, Giuseppe, Aliberti, Giovanni, in Bonuglia, Roberto (ed.), *Gioacchino Volpe tra passato e presente. Atti del convegno*, Roma, 1–2 dicembre 2005 (Rome: Aracne, 2007).
Cammarano, Fulvio (ed.), *Abbasso la guerra! Neutralisti in piazza alla vigilia della prima guerra mondiale in Italia* (Florence: Le Monnier, 2015).
Ceci, Lucia, *L'interesse superiore. Il Vaticano e l'Italia di Mussolini* (Rome-Bari: Laterza, 2013; English ed. 2017).
Chiurco, Giorgio Alberto, *Storia della rivoluzione fascista*, 5 vols (Florence: Vallecchi, 1929).
Crainz, Guido, *Padania. Il mondo dei braccianti dall'Ottocento alla fuga dalle campagne* (Rome: Donzelli, 1994).
Croce, Benedetto, *Per la nuova vita dell'Italia. Scritti e discorsi, 1934–1944* (Naples: Ricciardi, 1944).
De Felice, Renzo (ed.), *Il fascismo e i partiti politici italiani. Testimonianze del 1921–1923* (Florence: Le Lettere, 2005).
Dorso, Guido, *Mussolini alla conquista del potere* (Turin: Einaudi, 1949).
Farinacci, Roberto, *Storia della rivoluzione fascista*, 3 vols (Cremona: Cremona Nuova, 1937–1939).
Farinacci, Roberto, *Redenzione. Episodio cremonese della rivoluzione fascista. Dramma in tre atti* (Cremona: Cremona Nuova, 1927).
Fincardi, Marco, *Campagne emiliane in transizione* (Bologna: CLUEB, 2008).
Franzinelli, Mimmo, *Il filosofo in camicia nera. Giovanni Gentile e gli intellettuali di Mussolini* Milan: Mondadori, 2021).
Galfré, Monica, *Giuseppe Bottai. Un intellettuale fascista* (Florence: Giunti, 2000).
Gentile, Emilio, *E fu subito regime. Il fascismo e la marcia su Roma* (Rome-Bari: Laterza, 2012).
Gentile, Emilio, *Fascismo. Storia e interpretazione* (Rome-Bari: Laterza, 2002).
Gentile, Emilio, *Il mito dello Stato nuovo* (Rome-Bari: Laterza, 1999; 1st ed. 1982).
Gobetti, Piero, *La Rivoluzione Liberale. Saggio sulla lotta politica in Italia*, ed. by Ersilia Alessandrone Perona (Turin: Einaudi, 1995; 1st ed. Bologna: Cappelli, 1924).
Gramsci, Antonio, *Sul Risorgimento*, ed. by Elsa Fubini (Rome: Editori Riuniti, 1959).
Gramsci, Antonio, *Contro il populismo* (Villaricca: CentoAutori, 2019).
Gramsci, Antonio, *Sul fascismo*, introduction by Enzo Santarelli (Rome: Editori Riuniti, 1973).
Isnenghi, Mario and Albanese, Giulia (eds). *Gli italiani in guerra: conflitti, identità, memorie dal Risorgimento ai nostri giorni*, vol. 4.1, *Il ventennio fascista. Dall'impresa di Fiume alla seconda guerra mondiale, 1919–1940* (Turin: UTET, 2008).
Isnenghi, Mario, Ceschin, Daniele (eds), *Gli italiani in guerra: conflitti, identità, memorie dal Risorgimento ai nostri giorni*, vol. 3.1, *La Grande Guerra: dall'Intervento alla "vittoria mutilata"* (Turin: UTET, 2008).
Isnenghi, Mario. *L'Italia in piazza. I luoghi della vita pubblica dal 1848 ai giorni nostri* (Milan: Mondadori, 1994).
Lussu, Emilio, *Marcia su Roma e dintorni. Fascismo visto da vicino* (Paris: Critica, 1931; English ed.1992).
Manfredi, Marco, Papadia, Elena (eds), special issue on *Leader carismatici e movimenti sociali nell'Ottocento europeo*, in *Memoria e Ricerca*, n. 2, 2021.

Melloni, Alberto (ed.), *Benedict XV. A Pope in the World of the "Useless Slaughter" (1914–1918)*, 2 vols (Turnhout: Brepols, 2020; Italian ed. 2017).

Mussolini, Benito, *Il mio diario di guerra (1915–1917)*, ed. by Mario Isnenghi (Bologna: Il Mulino, 2016).

Nenni, Pietro, *Storia di quattro anni, 1919–1922. Crisi del dopoguerra e avvento del fascismo al potere*, ed. by Domenico Zucaro (Milan: Sugarco Edizioni, 1976; 1st ed., 1926).

Rosselli, Carlo, *Socialismo liberale* (Florence: Vallecchi, 1945; 1st ed. Paris 1930).

Rossi, Ernesto, *Il "Non Mollare"*, in *Il Ponte*, vol. 1, n. 6, 1945.

Salvatorelli, Luigi, *Nazionalfascismo*, foreword by Giorgio Amendola (Turin: Einaudi, 1977; 1st ed. Piero Gobetti 1923).

Salvemini, Gaetano, *Le origini del fascismo in Italia. Lezioni di Harvard* (Milan: Feltrinelli, 1979; 1st ed. 1961).

Silone, Ignazio, *Il fascismo. Origini e sviluppo* (Milan: Mondadori, 2002; 1st ed. Switzerland 1934).

Tamaro, Attilio, *Venti anni di storia: 1922–1943* (Rome: Tiber, 1953).

Tasca, Angelo, *Nascita e avvento del fascismo* (Bari: Laterza, 1965; first ed., Paris 1938; first Italian ed. Florence: La Nuova Italia, 1950; English ed. 2010).

Tesi di Lione, in Bartolotti, Mirella (ed.), *Le origini del fascismo* (Bologna: Zanichelli, 1969).

Togliatti, Palmiro, *Lezioni sul fascismo* (Rome: Editori Riuniti, 1970).

Treves, Claudio, *La Politica interna ed estera: Discorso nella tornata parlamentare 12 Luglio 1917* (Milan: Libreria Editrice Avanti!, 1917).

Turati, Filippo, *Per un'unica internazionale dei lavoratori*, in Schiavi, Alessandro, *Esilio e morte di Filippo Turati* (Rome: Opere Nuove, 1956).

Vacca, Giuseppe, *La tragica modernità del fascismo. Le analisi di Antonio Gramsci, Palmiro Togliatti e Angelo Tasca* (Rome: Carocci, 2022).

Volpe, Gioacchino. *Il popolo italiano tra la pace e la guerra* (Rome: Bonacci, 1992; 1st ed. 1940).

Volpe, Gioacchino, *Genesi del fascismo* (Rome: L'economia italiana, 1935).

CHAPTER 3

Coming to Terms with the Near Past: Post-war Historiography

Historical interpretations of fascism did not change substantially for about 15 years after the fall of the regime and the Liberation, as Renzo De Felice noted in 1969. Historians mostly concentrated on the origins of fascism, reflecting on a debate that had developed in the interwar period (De Felice 1969, pp. 193–194). There were cultural and practical interests that seemed more urgent: the new political forces attracted more interest than fascism, and they wanted to value their own history. What followed was a flourishing of research and studies on these post-war political protagonists, especially on the socialist workers' movement and the catholic movement. It was also difficult to access archival sources at that stage; and fascism was "too fresh a wound" to warrant historical study. Leaving aside fascist apologists such as Attilio Tamaro, prevailing interpretations in the 1940s and 1950s remained influenced by the "classical" analyses proposed under fascism (for example, Valeri 1956; De Rosa 1958). It would be unfair, however, to judge this outcome negatively, in part because the classical interpretations all retained aspects of historical truth, underlined the importance of certain components, and, taken together, revealed some of the complexities in the fascist phenomenon (Quazza 1973, pp. 5–6).

For several years, historians returned to analysing the themes of the previous debate: the importance of the First World War, the internal conflict of 1919–1922, the crisis of socialism and of the liberal state. From the 1960s more attention was devoted to the middle classes, and to major aspects of the dictatorship. Between the mid-1960s and the mid-1980s, new themes began to emerge through the debate, also surrounding interpretations advanced by De Felice. This debate took two different formats: a public one, very politicised and publicised by the media (newspapers, magazines and television), and one that developed in history books and academic journals. In particular, historians close to the Institutes for the History of the Resistance proposed new interpretations, often published in the journal linked to the institutes, *Italia*

Contemporanea (until 1974 entitled *Il Movimento di Liberazione in Italia*), founded in 1949, among others, by partisan leader and first Italian prime minister in 1945, Ferruccio Parri; from the 1960s, it became the first scholarly journal devoted to the history of twentieth-century Italy and in the first decades it became a fundamental repository of the research and debates on fascism and the Resistance. Scholarly work on fascism also appeared in other journals, which began to multiply in number, particularly from the later decades of the century.

POST-WAR RESEARCH ON THE ORIGINS OF FASCISM

In a book published in Italy in 1966, containing his lectures at Harvard during the Second World War, Salvemini dated the origins of fascism to the First World War (Salvemini 1966), following a tradition that can be found in the interpretations, among others, of Turati and Nenni (Turati 1945; Nenni 1926). The exiled historian argued that in May 1915, for the first time in Italian public life, there was the anomaly of a pseudo-revolutionary manifestation, favoured and even provoked by men who were in power, to force the will of parliament. In May 1915, prime minister Salandra and foreign minister Sidney Sonnino, supported by the interventionist groups, pursued a genuine coup against the parliamentary majority. In his view, this was practice for the next coup, in Rome in October 1922 (Salvemini 1966, p. 114). In a book published two years later, Marxist historian Giuliano Procacci, like Salvemini, emphasised that the transformation of the state began earlier than fascism: the state became authoritarian during the First World War even though parliament was still functioning, but met more seldom. There were even two governmental crises: in June 1916, after the Austrian offensive at the Asiago plateau, when Salandra was replaced by a national unity government led by Boselli; and in October 1917, after Caporetto, under liberal prime minister Orlando. However, in general, parliament had no control. The opposition, and especially the socialist press, was in no better state: newspapers were published with white columns because of the censorship. Punishment for those who were accused of being subversive or defeatist included house arrest or internal exile, all of which anticipated aspects of the fascist regime (Procacci 1968, pp. 489–490).

One of the most intelligent analyses of fascism during the post-war years was written by historian and former partisan (who had been close to the democratic Action Party) Federico Chabod, who partly incorporated the work of Nenni and Salvemini. About the pre-1914 situation, he confirmed that in terms of socio-economic development, political practice and cultural-psychological attitudes, and even in some practical manifestations, it was possible to find anticipations of fascism. However, it was not possible to attribute to these the character of "the seeds of fascism", an idea that developed later. Without the war, none of them might have developed any further, while opposite scenarios could have occurred. The crisis of May 1915, as Salvemini had also argued, opened the way to a path that would lead to fascism, but it was only in the post-war years that the crisis led to fascist success. Until the end of 1920, with the conclusion of the "red biennial", fascism had been a movement that could be overlooked (De Felice 1969, pp. 131–133; Tasca 1950; Chabod 1961).

The catholic world also participated in the debate. Sturzo, returned from exile, in 1957 wrote a book on the PPI that was also concerned with the causes of fascism. One context for the rise of fascism was the struggle in the Po valley, an area characterised by rich agriculture and well-developed technology with a higher population than any other region, one where the so-called "red domination" had become "unbearable". In his view, this was a class struggle, in which the fascists were on the side of the agrarians. A similar situation existed in the areas of the *mezzadria* (sharecropping), in Tuscany, Umbria and the Marche. In the cities, the liberal and conservative bourgeoisie was trying to wrest control of the communes and provinces from the socialists. Giolitti organised the 1921 elections to control the illegal armed fascists in order to encourage the socialists to collaborate, playing on the division between them and the communists, but also, Sturzo claimed, in the hope of curbing the PPI and reducing its numbers. The result did not meet his expectations: the socialist vote diminished slightly, but the PSI refused collaboration, the PPI's vote rose from 99 to 107, and the fascists, 35 of whom were elected as deputies, did not renounce their armed organisation, but intensified it against socialists, communists and *popolari* (PPI members). Under Giolitti, fascism was armed and militarily organised, and began to abandon its anti-clericalism and republicanism in order to endorse a union with liberal, conservatives and nationalists, even becoming pro-catholic in the process. Sturzo was clearly writing to defend the position of the PPI, as if it were the only party that bore no responsibility for the fascist victory. In his view, responsibility lay mostly with the ruling class that had, over the three years 1919–1922, tolerated all the violence and illegality, whether it came "in the name of nationalism, of socialism, or of fascism" (Sturzo 1957, pp. 87–90).

The help that fascism received from the conservative classes—the monarchy, the army, the Vatican and high finance—was crucial, according to the liberal historian Nino Valeri, writing in 1953. Fascism would have never achieved power simply as a result of its own leaders' strategy and the actions of the blackshirts. In his view, the old regime, crumbling from within, capitulated in confrontation with such "wild energy" that demonstrated complete contempt for the rules of civil life, adapting to a collaboration in which it appeared increasingly servile. After the generous but unpolitical attempt of the Aventine secession, the regime allowed itself to be absorbed by fascism (Valeri 1956, p. 754).

Most of the analyses explored so far found the reasons for fascism's success in the mistakes of the liberal state and its opponents, as well as the huge changes produced by the war. But from the 1960s, some historians began to also analyse the peculiarities of the Italian middle classes and their crucial support for fascism during the post-war years. According to Chabod, Giolitti failed to repeat with fascism the success he had had with socialism in the first 15 years of the century, when he broke its revolutionary impulse. The impression of government weakness that frightened the middle classes during the "red biennial" was real, and prefects, police functionaries and generals came from those classes: fascism obtained support from functionaries who preferred to close their eyes to fascist excesses rather than enforce the law (Chabod 1961, pp. 67; 72). Chabod also paid attention to the groups of ex-combatants that surrounded Mussolini in 1919, who were moved by a feeling of revolt against political forces both within and outside Italy that seemed to humiliate the fatherland. Many of them withdrew support once they saw fascism turning into a dictatorship; for example, in 1925 the National Association of Combatants asked for the king's intervention against Mussolini. But for some of them the psychological impact of war weighed heavily, making the return to civilian life intolerable. Others, like Farinacci, had not even fought in the war, but had a spirit of adventure and a will for social climbing. The petit bourgeoisie, ex-officers and students who gathered around Mussolini did so mainly out of offended national sentiment, but they also feared revolution. These groups were not intellectually astute enough to understand that the hopes for revolution in Italy had ended after September 1920. For Chabod, it was possible to explain fascism not only as a reaction by industrialists and agrarians against the left, but as a result of challenges to patriotic sentiment (Chabod 1961, p. 62).

Here it is useful to consider the views of De Felice. For him it was fundamental to consider fascism in the chronological, historical, and geographical context within which it developed. The fascist outcome from the interwar period was not inevitable, nor the result of necessity. It was the consequence of a multiplicity of contingent and explicable factors, of illusions, mistakes and fears, and, for a minority, of determination. An important element of analysis for De Felice concerned the social basis of fascism. He agreed with historian and philosopher Croce that fascism found supporters and opponents in all social classes, but also with the German psychoanalyst Erich Fromm, who observed that, while the working class and the liberal and catholic bourgeoisie generally had a negative or resigned view of fascism, its main supporters were to be found from among the middle classes. The link with the middle classes was one of the main aspects of fascism at the time of its seizure of power, but also later in the dictatorship. On a psychological-political level, the crisis of the middle classes manifested itself in a state of social frustration that became translated into a state of profound agitation, a confused desire for revenge against a society that they felt victimised them. In these terms, fascism would have represented a third way between parliamentary democracy and communism (De Felice 1969).

Historians also devoted attention to fascism's "first year", developing research in the field for many years up to and including the recent work by Mimmo Franzinelli (2019). Valeri was among the first, reflecting on the events of 1919 when fascism tried to unify the two great contemporary currents of nationalism and socialism (a widespread desire also experienced outside Italy), but failed. The fascist failure in 1919 was not in question: in the November elections they obtained only a few thousand votes in Milan. And for the whole year, and a great part of 1920, the fascists did not move out from the urban centres, where they confronted united masses of workers, strengthened by the autonomy they had obtained after a long tradition of trade union battles. It was necessary, Valeri continued, to remember that fascism did not exhaust itself entirely in armed defence of conservative economic and financial forces, but retained part of its original radical impulse. The first fascists showed a determination to run any risk to avoid returning to a normal daily life; they displayed a desperate anger at a government that had betrayed them at Versailles, at the new rich who had made money "out of their blood", at the proletariat that had opposed the war and was now triumphant and economically strengthened, and at a state elite that they perceived as tired and incapable (Valeri 1956, p. 756).

In another important contribution, Procacci located the origins of fascism in the general context of 1919—a year in which the whole world of work was in turmoil. Those enrolled in trade unions in their hundreds of thousands before the war were now in their millions. Strikes involved not only factory workers, who obtained higher wages and the eight-hour working day, but also railway workers, postal workers, peasants of the Po valley and sharecroppers of central Italy, and even ministerial white-collar employees. In the countryside of Lazio and southern Italy the peasants occupied the land and forced landowners to accept the *fait accompli*. In June, many cities were theatres of violent agitation against high prices, assuming in some cases the character of insurrection. D'Annunzio's occupation of Fiume in September, with the acquiescence of the army authorities, was the first instance of the subversion of the state from the right that would culminate in the march on Rome, but it was welcomed by parts of the left as a symptom of a revolutionary situation, and it demonstrated that the seeds of insubordination against the state authorities had reached army ranks (Procacci 1968, p. 494).

Among the new post-war writing on the rise of fascism, the theory developed by socialists and communists in the interwar years of fascism as the armed reaction of industrial and agrarian capitalism was revived. The Marxist philosopher Antonio Banfi observed in 1960 that Italy and Germany both experienced a revival of capitalism after the First World War, in countries where democracy lacked deep roots. What allowed fascism and National Socialism to seize power was the collusion between *squadrismo* and capitalism. Militant fascism and capitalism were not a united entity: in their social origins and interests they remained two distinct and cooperating forces, but with capitalism as the dominant one. The destruction of the trade unions, strike-breaking, suppression of the socialist and communist parties, and the persecution of their representatives were acts in which the interests of fascism and capitalism coincided, and were the basis for the stabilisation of the totalitarian regime (Banfi 1960, pp. 241–250).

The defeat of socialism was something that Procacci also addressed. On the one hand, Nicola Bombacci, Costantino Lazzari, Giacinto Menotti Serrati and other maximalist leaders kept postponing the revolution that they seemed to consider inevitable; on the other, Turati and the reformists did not want to take responsibility in a shared government with the bourgeoisie. The Turin factory council movement was certainly the vanguard of the Italian revolutionary movement, but as such it could be easily isolated and defeated. In September 1920 steel workers occupied their factories, protecting them with weapons while flying red flags from the rooftops, and for a few days it looked as if the revolution had finally started. Giolitti understood that the socialist and trade union leaders would not take this further and there was no real possibility of a revolutionary outcome, so instead obtained a compromise. The communist secession from the PSI in 1921 was followed in October 1922 by a reformist breakaway (with the foundation of the *Partito Socialista Unitario* by, among others, Turati, Matteotti and Treves), so that at the advent of fascism, Procacci continued, the "old glorious socialist party" was divided in three sections. The economic crisis, instead of generating revolution, spawned reaction: the Italian situation of 1921–1922 constituted in many ways an anticipation of the situation that developed in Germany just before the seizure of power by Nazism. It was a "provincial civil war", with all the partisanship and fury of provincial wars, but, above all, it was a class war conducted by extreme means. The success of the punitive expeditions and the fascist raids would not have been possible, however, without the complicity of the army and of the government (Procacci 1968, p. 501). These were all views that had much in common with the political and social analyses of the pre-war years.

Renzo De Felice's Biography of Mussolini and Its Impact: The Early Years

A turning-point in the post-war discussion of fascism and its leader came in the mid-1960s with the publication of the first volume of Renzo De Felice's monumental biography of Mussolini. De Felice was active as a historian from the mid-1960s to the mid-1990s, during which he produced eight volumes of the biography, for a total of around 7000 pages, published by Einaudi. Despite a long-winded and contorted writing style, a large documentary apparatus and extended footnotes, it enjoyed a huge commercial success, with a number of reprints until the 2000s (one undertaken by the right-wing newspaper *Il Giornale*) and even in CD Rom format for popular magazines such as *TV Sorrisi e Canzoni* and *Panorama*. In the 1960s he published *Mussolini il rivoluzionario, 1883–1920* (Mussolini the revolutionary, in 1965), *Mussolini il fascista. La conquista del potere, 1921–1925* (Mussolini the fascist: The conquest of power, in 1966), *Mussolini il fascista. L'organizzazione dello Stato fascista, 1925–1929* (Mussolini the fascist: The organisation of the fascist state, in 1968). Two volumes on Mussolini the *duce*, one on the "years of consensus" and one on "the totalitarian state", appeared respectively in 1974 and 1981: *Mussolini il Duce. Gli anni del consenso, 1929–1936* and *Mussolini il Duce. Lo Stato totalitario, 1936–1940*. The years of the Second World War were covered in the 1990s, with two volumes on "Mussolini the ally" on the fascist war,

Mussolini l'alleato. L'Italia in guerra, 1940–1943 (1990) and one final volume, published in 1997, one year after De Felice's death, on the "civil war": *Mussolini l'alleato. La guerra civile, 1943–1945*. He also edited anthologies of writings about fascism, wrote prefaces and introductions, and participated in the public discourse on fascism with many interviews, some collected as volumes and a large number appeared in both the daily and popular press. This was a vast body of work that prompted wide and polemical debate, not only among historians but also the wider public, particularly in the 1980s and early 1990s.

The first phase of De Felice's biography of Mussolini focused on the years preceding the establishment of the regime. Between 1965 and 1968, before publishing his book on the interpretations of fascism in 1969, De Felice produced the first three volumes of the biography at a time when themes devoted to the war, the post-war crisis and the origins of fascism were at the centre of historical writing. In the 1960s De Felice focused on Mussolini as a socialist and on his trajectory from socialism to fascism at the time of the crisis of the liberal state. One innovative aspect of his research was the attention paid to the cult of Mussolini as a socialist. De Felice did not simply interpret him from the perspective of what occurred later, but inserted Mussolini firmly into the socialist tradition of charismatic leadership as part of the history of the cultural and social currents of Italian socialism. In particular, he reconstructed Mussolini's political trajectory as editor of the PSI's national newspaper, *Avanti!*, from 1912, and as one of the most important leaders of the party at the head of the intransigent revolutionary group (De Felice 1965, pp. 176–177). Similarly, Mussolini's conversion to interventionism was not reduced to political opportunism and funding from industrialists and French financiers (which arrived after his conversion, with the publication of *Il Popolo d'Italia*, and not before), but was placed in the context of similar choices made by other revolutionary left-wing leaders and intellectuals.

These interpretations were to be shared and developed further by later historiography. The historian and former pupil of De Felice, Giovanni Sabbatucci later suggested that De Felice's argument supporting the existence of a myth of "revolutionary war" was less well-grounded, as it seemed implausible that interventionists could have conducted a revolutionary war "under the flags of the king and under Cadorna's command" (Sabbatucci in Chessa-Villari 2002, p. 81). De Felice himself was indeed aware that the myth had no bearing on reality because the masses (both catholic and socialist) did not follow left-wing interventionism but remained neutralist (De Felice 1965, p. 296). He also explored the world of left-wing interventionism, revealing a political context previously largely ignored, one that historians would later define as radical nationalism, linked with the mobilisation of the middle classes, a world where the borders between right and left became indistinct.

In the 1960s and 1970s De Felice established a fruitful relationship with the catholic philosopher Augusto Del Noce, who was also opposed to the idea of fascism as simply a reactionary, barbarian and authoritarian movement interested only in the defence of the past. He emphasised the influence both of futurism and revolutionary syndicalism in the first wave of fascism (Del Noce 1970, in Del Noce 1995, p. 43). But could Mussolini be described as a revolutionary, and until when? The title of De Felice's first volume, *Mussolini the Revolutionary*, which covered the years up to 1920, attracted much criticism. "Revolutionary" was a term used to define the left, so Mussolini's support for the Italian intervention in the war and his violent attacks against the socialist and neutralist left during and after the war years could be better defined as "subversive" (Sabbatucci in Chessa and Villari 2002, p. 82). In his second volume, *Mussolini the Fascist*, De Felice went on to explain further his view that fascism was not simply born of the nationalist right, but was one of the many products of left-wing interventionism. In his view, Mussolini's fascism was "a dynamic fact", different from agrarian fascism, which was a reaction in favour of a particular class of landowners without political prospects (De Felice 1966, p. 16). This distinction has been partly revised by recent historiography on *squadrismo*, which showed how landowners themselves often founded local *fasci* and squads, or were at their head, and were therefore integral to the fascist project, rather than simply fellow travellers (Franzinelli 2003, p. 68). Although Mussolini founded fascism as an urban reality, just as interventionism had been, De Felice acknowledged that he would never reject the fundamental help received from agrarian *squadrismo*, which allowed him to win his anti-Bolshevik battle (De Felice 1966, p. 16). The persistence of a left-wing interventionism into the post-war years is also debatable, as, particularly after the defeat at Caporetto, different forms of interventionism began to blend together into defence of the fatherland and a violent assault against socialism and neutralism, so from that point on left-wing interventionism had become difficult to distinguish from that of the nationalist right (Baldoli 2002, p. 40).

De Felice also developed the idea that Mussolini's political culture had its roots in the historic left, with links to the French Revolution and the Risorgimento, and not in the reactionary right, as he thought was the case with Hitler (although most historians now see Hitler as a radical nationalist, not part of the old right in Germany). The young Mussolini, like many of his generation, mixed revolutionary ideas with national sentiment. As the historian and Mussolini's biographer Pierre Milza noted in 2002 in a collective reassessment of De Felice's work, Mussolini was indeed brought up in that culture and adapted to all its ambiguities. As De Felice had argued, at the beginning of the twentieth century there was a revision of Marxism, from both the right and the left, in view of the incapacity of the socialist parties to bring about a revolution. The readings of Friedrich Nietzsche, Sorel and Vilfredo Pareto promoted the idea of the "new man" forged in violent struggle, and rejection of the positivism and humanism of the democratic model. What resulted was an encounter between some of the revolutionary syndicalists with nationalist intellectuals, such as those who wrote in the journals *Leonardo* (founded by Giovanni Papini in 1903) and *La Voce* (founded by Giuseppe Prezzolini in 1908). They supported the idea of the primacy of a spiritual and civilising mission in Italy. The war became the opportunity for the affirmation of a new revolutionary elite, which began to replace the concept of class with that of nation, and opposed the neutralist and internationalist socialist party with increasing violence. In 1918 Mussolini changed the subtitle of *Il Popolo d'Italia* from "socialist daily" to "daily of combatants and producers", and certainly by then Mussolini was clearly no longer a socialist, nor a Marxist (which he probably had never been). He saw himself as a new type of revolutionary, whose aim was not to give power to the proletariat but to replace the old hierarchy with a new one; capitalism was not the enemy, on the contrary it participated in the common good and the greatness of the nation. During the war years it was therefore possible to see elements of the future official ideology of the fascist regime: the myth of revolution, the nation as a supreme value, the collaboration between classes as an instrument of national cohesion, an elite of combatants and producers, all of which was to be directed by the state. Mussolini thus shared with part of the war generation this political culture that moved from the extreme left to fascism: a double culture, both revolutionary and national (Milza in Chessa and Villari 2002, pp. 111–136).

The economic historian Valerio Castronovo contributed to this debate by investigating the relationship between Italy's big industrial groups and fascism, beginning with the First World War years. While the support of industrialists for Mussolini in 1919—despite the demagogic character of the San Sepolcro programme—should not be used to simplify fascism as merely the "agent of capital", it still provides a challenge to the idea of Mussolini as a "revolutionary" (Castronovo in Quazza 1973, p. 57).

Another interpretation by De Felice was presented in an interview with one of his collaborators at the University of Rome in the 1970s, the right-wing American historian (close to the Reagan administration in the 1980s), Michael Ledeen. He argued that it was possible to distinguish, within the fascist regime, a "fascism-movement", which preserved the revolutionary ideals of the San Sepolcro programme of 1919, from a "fascism-regime", a state that retained continuities with the era of Giolitti and the monarchy (De Felice 1975, pp. 28–29). In this way, the fascist regime still appeared to have roots in the left, and could be shorn of its totalitarian features. However, the fact that Mussolini and part of the fascist hierarchies had been from the beginning the bearers of a left-wing political culture did not make fascism a "left-wing" totalitarian regime. It was a reactionary regime based on the involvement of the masses, and in that sense, it is possible to trace many similarities with the National Socialist regime in Germany. After 1922, indeed, very little was left of Mussolini's original political culture. As we shall see, De Felice's refusal to compare Italian fascism and German Nazism was one aspect later contested by historians. For De Felice, it was fundamental to consider fascism in the actual chronological, historical, and geographical context within which it developed, which meant avoiding any general theory of fascism outside interwar Italy. Instead, very fruitful research has been published in the last decades on fascism's transnational and comparative dimensions.

THE QUESTION OF CONSENSUS

In the first part of his third volume, *Mussolini il Duce*, published in 1974, De Felice argued that fascism achieved a form of mass consensus among the Italian population particularly between 1929 and 1936. By 1929, he argued, fascism appeared to have acquired definite traits, while the Lateran Pacts (the agreement between the Holy See and the Kingdom of Italy, signed in that year by cardinal Gasparri and by Mussolini) had concluded a first phase of government, and sanctioned the structure of the regime in power. Despite some contradictions within the fascist elite itself, the regime could boast a solidity based on mass consensus. It was a consensus that implied a general depoliticisation, increasingly detached from the fascist party, based largely on the cult of Mussolini and on the idea that he had remade Italy (De Felice 1974, p. 3). A majority of Italians did not question state authority despite a period of economic crisis, rising unemployment and falling wage-levels. A huge propaganda project contributed to creating this climate of consensus; for example, great success came from the reclamation of the Pontine marshes and the creation of new towns such as Littoria and Sabaudia (De Felice 1974, pp. 65–66; p. 124). The conquest of Ethiopia and the mobilisation against the economic sanctions imposed by the League of Nations led to a state of exaltation and collective enthusiasm in 1935–1936. The catholic Church contributed to the orientation of public opinion, aligning itself with the regime. In terms of support for the regime from the clergy and a vast majority of catholics, the conquest of Ethiopia took it to levels that would not be achieved again, claimed De Felice, even during the Spanish Civil War (De Felice 1974, p. 623; p. 762). It was the first time that fascism was studied not simply as an oppressive dictatorship, but as a regime based on popular support, raising an issue that has continued to be debated into the twenty-first century.

Historians of Italian catholicism have shown that the support of the Vatican was instrumental in creating the consensus. Initial exploration by Pietro Scoppola and Giovanni Miccoli demonstrated how support for the regime was part of the historical development of the Church, which had begun to cooperate with Italian governments from the time of the pontificate of Leo XIII (pope between 1878 and 1903). The Church was motivated by anti-socialist and anti-subversive sentiment, but also by its experience during the First World War, when the clergy and catholic organisations provided aid for the military effort (Miccoli in Quazza 1973, p. 188). The relationship between Church and state remained one of collaboration during fascism, despite moments of tension (Scoppola 1976, p. 67). The Church in Italy during fascism became progressively entrenched in an ethical-political conception that reduced the duties of citizens to respect for state authority (consistently with St. Paul's teachings), so that any attempt by catholics to oppose fascism was quashed under the moral and religious judgement of the Vatican (Scoppola and Traniello 1975, p. 10). Behind the adhesion of a large part of the catholic world to fascism was the conservative class that had previously helped to bring the Church close to the liberal leadership, which was seen as the saviour of property and social order (Miccoli in Quazza 1973, p. 195).

There were also important reflections on the question of consensus at the end of the 1970s from the cultural historian Mario Isnenghi. According to Isnenghi, it was crucial to investigate the question of the relationship between coercion and consensus in order to move away from the idea of a regime rejected by a few heroes and accepted out of convenience by everyone else, particularly in the age of the masses, when governments sought to establish a relationship between citizens and state based on a myth of participation. After the war, the Italian middle classes had allowed the development of a discourse about fascist Italy as "an empty church, without religion and without faithful": a representation of Italian fascism and of the average Italian that was as stereo-typed as the image projected by the fascist regime, of a compact and convinced fascist country (Isnenghi 1979 [1], p. 20). The difficulties experienced by historiography in coming to terms with the question of consensus was one of the effects—and one of the causes—of such a collective need to repress memory. Consequently, argued Isnenghi, a historical landscape emerged of a fascism without fascists, in which everyone, industrialists and catholics, military personnel and monarchists, bourgeois and proletarians, "exchange mutual historical absolutions, testimonies of having acted out of permanent necessity and falsehood". However, a political project that aspired to be totalitarian and not simply to manage power, could not succeed without a consistent body of people that elaborated and disseminated in society the symbols and ideological motivations that legitimised power (Isnenghi 1979 [1], pp. 21–22; 24).

In 1981, Giulio Sapelli added that in order to measure consensus, it was necessary to make class distinctions. He found that it was inappropriate to use the concept of consensus to describe the relationship between the working classes and fascism in what was effectively a reactionary mass regime that had repressed and deleted any political and social autonomy of the worker's movement by manipulating the masses from above: how was it possible, he asked, to deduce consensus from the participation of workers in the fascist unions, the afterwork organisations or the public ceremonies? The consensus was a complex question that needed a serious and scientific investigation (Sapelli 1981, p. ix–xcviii). As we shall see, the historiography of fascism until today has continued to develop answers to these challenging issues.

A Totalitarian regime? The Origins of a Long-term Debate

The question of whether fascism in Italy established, or sought to establish, a totalitarian regime, together with the debate on the general category of totalitarianism, was already a live issue under fascism itself, although a discussion based on the examination of primary sources only began between the 1960s and the 1970s. Many differing opinions have been presented in the decades since. The most negative assessments, which deny that fascism in Italy was ever totalitarian, are largely based on a comparison with Nazi Germany. The first and most famous of these was advanced in 1951 by the German political philosopher Hannah Arendt, who compared Mussolini's Italy with Hitler's Germany and Stalin's Soviet Union. According to her, although totalitarianism was part of Mussolini's rhetoric, the Italian dictator never tried to establish a perfect totalitarianism and only succeeded in realising a one-party dictatorship (Arendt 2021, pp. 427–428). In her view, the essence of a totalitarian state was the existence of mass terror and mass extermination, which were fully applied only in Nazi Germany and the Soviet Union. Italian fascism was consequently compared to traditional dictatorships led by generals or bureaucrats without a mass party, a point of view that, according to the historian Gentile, was caused by Arendt's lack of knowledge of Italy's historical, political, institutional, social, and cultural reality: her only historical sources were a few discourses by Mussolini and a leaflet from the Italian confederation of industrialists (Gentile 1995, p. 66).

However, Arendt's work was very influential, even among scholars such as De Felice and Alberto Aquarone. In 1965 a crucial intervention in this debate was published by Aquarone on the "organisation of the totalitarian state", which argued that under fascism the totalitarian state—as a form of total integration of the society into the state—was never realised. This was principally because, despite Mussolini's totalitarian aspirations, the dictator was never able to resolve the problem of fascism's relationship to the monarchy and the catholic Church: the result was a fascist state that remained a dynastic and catholic state until its end (Aquarone 1965, p. 291). Despite the fact that, from the march on Rome until July 1943, Victor Emmanuel III never obstructed any of Mussolini's actions and endorsed every fascist law—providing his support after the murder of Matteotti all the way through to the invasion of Ethiopia, the racist laws of 1938 and Italy's declaration of war against France and Britain in 1940—according to Aquarone, the totalitarian state could not be realised with an army that was loyal to the monarchy rather than to fascism, a loyalty that was also true for some party officials (Aquarone 1965, p. 292). As we shall see, the relationship between fascism and the military leadership has recently come under closer scrutiny, demonstrating a deeper "fascistisation" of the armed forces.

More than the monarchy, it was the catholic Church that had profound roots in Italian society and significant influence among the Italian masses. With the Lateran Pacts of 1929, fascism largely succeeded in using the Church to increase its prestige and strengthen its position within Italy and abroad, while at the same time the regime relinquished any attempt to determine the spiritual education of Italians, accepting the partition of spheres of influence with the Church—a compromise that was probably inevitable for Mussolini, given the strength of the competitor. Particularly in rural areas and the provinces, it was often the cross rather than the fascist lictors that informed public life and won devotion—a situation that infuriated many local fascist leaders who had never abandoned the anti-clericalism of early fascism, and who found the competition from local bishops unacceptable (Aquarone 1965, p. 293; p. 296). Moreover, large industrial, financial, and agrarian power had always retained an essentially instrumental conception of fascism, which implied support, but not unconditionally, and not total identification. Fascism achieved close association with the middle classes, who were attracted by its violent nationalism and anti-socialism; however, even in this case, the material advantages remained limited and insufficient to accept personal sacrifice—especially with reference to the regime's military enterprises. This meant that convinced adhesion to fascism at some point became a form of passive acceptance (Aquarone 1965, p. 300).

The main criticism of Aquarone's interpretation of fascist totalitarianism came later from Gentile, who remarked how terms such as "totalitarian", "totalitarianism" and "total dictatorship" were used for the first time by anti-fascist intellectuals and politicians between 1923 and 1925 in order to expose the reality of fascism in action and the consequences of those actions: these included the suppression of all political parties, the end of democratic political culture, the absolute control of administrative and political life, the monopolisation of people's consciousness (acting as a form of religion with liturgical rituals), the idea of purifying violence, and the sanctity of the fatherland. Democratic political opponents such as Dorso, Amendola and Salvatorelli thus laid the foundations for a long-term debate, and predated the use of the term by the fascists themselves, who appropriated it in 1925 to define a new concept of politics and the state. Anti-fascist and anti-communist intellectuals in the 1930s, not only Italians, elaborated on the concept with reference to fascist Italy, Nazi Germany, and Soviet Russia: all were regarded as single-party regimes founded on terror and demagogy, involving the masses in rituals and organisations, imposing their ideology as mass political religion. As Gentile noted, Arendt ignored those intellectuals and that debate entirely. His critique of Arendt, Aquarone and De Felice, dealt with more fully in the next chapter, was structured most definitively in his 1995 work on the "Italian road to totalitarianism".

The Conquest of Power

One way into the debate on totalitarianism is to assess how fascism conquered power in the 1920s. Here one of the most influential books, published in English in 1973, was Adrian Lyttleton's analysis of the seizure of power, translated into Italian as *La conquista del potere* a year later. This was a particularly difficult time for Italian democracy, when the left-wing movement born in the youth rebellion of 1968 was countered by a neo-fascist revival and terrorist massacres in the so-called "strategy of tension". The confrontation involved sections of the Italian state and the Italian and American secret services (Cuzzi et al. 2022). As a result, historians in the 1970s welcomed a volume that provided a contribution to the knowledge of what was still a recent—and still dauntingly alive—past. One reason for the interest provoked by Lyttleton's book, which both engaged with Italian historiography (especially from the 1960s) and presented new archival research, was that it was not concerned so much with the origins of fascism, but with its conquest of power and the development of the regime up to the Lateran Pacts of 1929. He argued that there were two principal reasons for fascism's success: at its origins, the lack of ideological cohesion that made it open to opportunistic changes became a point of strength; and, from the autumn of 1920, the transformation from an urban to an agrarian movement, with a strengthening of its reactionary character. This interpretation did not, however, imply recognition of an early revolutionary nature for fascism favoured by De Felice. Both urban and rural fascism shared a fundamental anti-socialist matrix; and the success of agrarian reaction was due to its links with a reactionary movement of the urban middle classes (Lyttelton 1974, p. 97). Lyttelton's view of the march on Rome was one of the first serious analyses that saw it as neither a revolution, as purported by the fascists, nor as a simple choreographic operation, but an example of a "psychological war" that succeeded in disorientating sections of the Italian state, the high command of the armed forces and the monarchy (Lyttelton 1974, p. 138).

As Marco Palla underlined in a review (Palla 1974), the most important aspect of Lyttelton's book was, however, the examination of the relationship between state and party, which built on Aquarone, who had limited his work to juridical-political aspects, and on De Felice, who had insisted on the general point that Mussolini consciously dismissed the party to amplify his own role as leader and statesman. Instead, for Lyttelton, fascism distinguished itself from traditional authoritarian states precisely through the active role of the party in the conquest of power, even though he conceded that later developments slowed the tendencies towards establishing an efficient totalitarian regime based on the party as the dominant institution. Anticipating recent research on the subject, Lyttelton was attentive to the relationship between the party and peripheral state administration, providing a first reconstruction of the roles of local fascist leaders who dominated provincial politics, and of their relationship with local capitalism—not only agrarian, but also financial (Lyttelton 1974, pp. 269–283). The subordination of the party to the state took place after 1926, following the complete elimination of all political organisations in Italy, when the duty of political control and repression was entrusted to the political police under Arturo Bocchini's leadership. However, in an analysis taking Florence as a case study, Lyttelton underlined the persistence of the party in sport and welfare organisations, which characterised its consolidation in the 1930s and defined fascism as a new type of reactionary regime (Lyttelton 1974, pp. 483–495). His work laid the foundations for later research on the relationship between party and state and those between the centre and the provinces.

FASCIST CULTURE AND IDEOLOGY

In his discussion of totalitarianism, Aquarone claimed that fascism failed to penetrate the world of the intelligentsia; fascism, he argued, was incapable of producing its own culture while the most distinguished intellectuals remained anti-fascist (Aquarone 1965, p. 301). Norberto Bobbio reinforced that position some eight years later in a contribution specifically devoted to the world of culture and fascism. He argued that in the process of the transformation of the state, academic culture did not undergo any major changes: it did not produce massive support, nor did it rebel—for example, academics mostly adapted, conformed, "curled up", in order to continue their work more or less undisturbed. At the beginning of the academic year 1931–1932, when an oath of loyalty to the regime was imposed on academics, only 12 out of 1200 refused to comply; the real moment of rupture came only with the racist laws in 1938, which excluded from the profession the numerous Jewish teachers (Bobbio in Quazza 1973, p. 214).

The continuity in Italian academia was also evident in the greatest cultural enterprise of fascism, the *Italian Encyclopaedia*, published between 1929 and 1937, with contributions from academics such as Chabod, Walter Maturi, Delio Cantimori, Guido Calogero, Luigi Russo, Mario Fubini, and Natalino Sapegno, the *crème de la crème* of post-war academic culture. Among the contributors to the *Encyclopaedia* were 90 authors who had signed a Manifesto of anti-fascist intellectuals promoted by Croce in 1925. The only important entries that were authentically fascist were those about fascism itself, its history, and its doctrine, written mostly by Giovanni Gentile (the regime's principal philosopher, ministry of education between 1922 and 1924) and Volpe, the nationalist historian who adhered to fascism in 1921. And, finally, Bobbio came to the controversial question: "The other reason why, despite examples of individual yielding, culture was not entirely fascistised, is to be found in the fact that a fascist culture ... had never really existed, or at least never managed, despite the efforts of the regime, to take shape into lasting and historically relevant initiatives". Even the young Gentilians who gathered around fascist journalist, jurist and intellectual Giuseppe Bottai only lasted a short time (Bobbio in Quazza 1973, p. 216; p. 229).

This view began to be thoroughly revised by the historian Luisa Mangoni, who produced a seminal book that scrutinised the fascist press and intellectuals from the pre-fascist years to the Second World War. She highlighted the role played by Bottai in the organisation of fascist culture from the period of the march on Rome. In attempting to identify fascism with the state, Bottai drew on a fully Italian tradition in order to counter Giolittian culture, and he found its roots in Gentile's anti-positivism and in nationalism (Mangoni 1974, pp. 66–67). Mangoni's work provided an analysis of fascist cultural magazines such as *Novecento*, *Selvaggio*, *Critica fascista* and *L'Universale*, demonstrating the different currents within the regime concerning the role of the party, fascist radicalism, fascist catholicism, ideas around revolution or normalisation, and the relationship with capitalism. In conclusion, historiography had to come to terms with the fact that a fascist culture *did* exist. She was writing in a decade when historians began to pay attention to features of everyday life in fascist Italy.

Another pioneer was once again Isnenghi, who opened the way to aspects of fascist history that would now be classified under the term "cultural studies".

He characterised not only the official culture of the regime but also the impact it had on Italian society. The cultural project of the regime involved a great many Italians, not only the few well-known ones, but also a myriad of lesser intellectuals, journalists, teachers at all educational levels, film directors, censors, librarians, publishers, orators and broadcasters, priests, and artists (Isnenghi 1979 [1], p. 4). Whether it concerned primary school textbooks or radio programmes, the question was: how much of all this influenced the average person, their emotions and their collective memory? What was the impact of the squares crowded with people after the conquest of the empire, of the rituals maintained in churches all over Italy "to sanctify wars of aggression into wars of religion", or of the monuments to the unknown soldier and the fallen of the "revolution" in every small village? (Isnenghi 1979 [1], pp. 5–6). Isnenghi wrote that, "the regime talked and continuously produced talks about itself"; it was, in great part, a "creation of words", but they were words that could become facts, or which the regime pretended could become facts (Isnenghi 1979 [2], p. 8). The regime controlled from the centre the instruments of propaganda, such as schools, the press, the radio, employees' clubs, and cinema, while at the same time it could count on the activism of a myriad of centres of cultural activity at the periphery. This represented a level of militancy and ideological participation that was higher than it had been with any previous Italian government (Isnenghi 1979 [2], p. 9). In this sense, culture did not just mean the presence of the great names of Italian literature, but was an expression of a fascist world view and the means for its dissemination.

Until the 1970s, historiography similarly showed little interest to the study of fascist ideology. The prevailing conviction was that fascism did not possess a precise ideology, but borrowed ideas from other political groups, mainly the nationalists, or developed different ideologies depending on the changing course of action and opportunity. If fascism had an ideology, it was not organic or coherent, but was continually improvised. Without denying the aspects of truth in these propositions, and without identifying fascism only with its ideology (on the contrary, understanding that ideology was only one of many aspects that could define fascism), Emilio Gentile in 1975 began to explore the subject-matter in greater depth. He started by investigating Mussolini's ideas and the way they were formed when he was a revolutionary socialist. Like many revolutionary syndicalists, such as Sorel, Mussolini was influenced not only by Marxism but also by Nietzsche, a prophet of the superman, of revolt against the bourgeois world, of violent action, and the rejection of rules and parliamentary democracy. He was also influenced by the sociologist Pareto, particularly his conception of a socialism based on a chosen minority and of history being always a history of minorities (Gentile 1975, p. 7; p. 13). According to Gentile, Mussolini was already "slipping out of socialism" well before the First World War (Gentile 1975, p. 28); the revisionist ideas he absorbed were ingredients of his later fascist ideology.

The other important ideological influence came with the war and the post-war climate, particularly from the currents of *combattentismo* (combat culture).

The ex-servicemen's movements turned their participation in the conflict into a claim to power and the right to remake Italy, a country they saw as corrupted by the world of the conservative bourgeoisie, socialist neutralists, catholic pacifists, and all those who gained economic advantage from the war. Among the educated petit bourgeoisie that had provided the army with officers, *combattentismo* provided both an ideology and a moral outlook. Mussolini's *Il Popolo d'Italia* became the mouthpiece for their aspirations and contributed to the dissemination of "those antiparliamentary and anti-party motives that were the embryonic focal point of fascist ideology" (Gentile 1975, p. 74).

Gentile identified another element in the evolution of fascist ideology in the views of Agostino Lanzillo, a syndicalist, follower of Sorel and later fascist, who argued that both socialism and capitalism were in crisis and anticipated the doctrine of the "third way". The latter idea was incorporated into the fascist corporative ideology; although it was never fully implemented in practice, fascism continued to refer to corporatism, and many fascists believed (or wanted to believe) in the idea. According to Lanzillo, a new ideology would be born from the post-war situation that was not democratic, egalitarian, pacifist, or rationalist, but instead was nationalist and hierarchical. These ideas were shared by another important ideological influence, futurism, a movement that condemned bourgeois materialism, ignored the question of social classes, only recognised the qualities of "genius" in any claim to power, and was both anti-parliamentarian and anti-democratic (Gentile 1975, pp. 77–79; p. 113).

In 1920 some of the most heterodox propositions of 1919 fascism—particularly the republican and anti-Vatican stance—were abandoned. The character of fascist membership was changing, mainly due to the support of the agrarian class, and following the 1921 elections, when 35 fascists entered parliament. These transformations, Gentile argued, did not alter aspects of the initial ideology, which were manifested during the regime: the glorification of war as a revolutionary moment, the myth of *combattentismo*, the contempt for democracy, the exaltation of nationalist sentiment, the social vindication of the middle classes, the myth of hierarchy. It was necessary to add a new ideology of the state to these ideas, as fascism turned into a regime (Gentile 1975, pp. 325–326).

Here, an important contribution was made by philosopher Giovanni Gentile's idealism—with its spiritualism, anti-materialism, anti-positivism, and anti-democratic elements. Gentile's most important follower and one of the fascist regime's intellectuals, Ugo Spirito, defined fascism as "the first political manifestation of the new idealistic thought" (Gentile 1975, p. 331; p. 341). For Giovanni Gentile, fascism was a political phenomenon that expressed the will of the masses to participate in the life of the state and the nation. He synthesized fascist ideology as both the inheritance and the transcendence of the nineteenth century national political movements, a completion of the project of the Risorgimento. Another fascist intellectual, Sergio Panunzio, developed the idea of fascist corporatism within the new regime. He argued that the fascist trade unions should form the heart of the state, but this piece of fascist ideology was never seriously implemented, since trade unions could only retain a subordinate function in an authoritarian state (Gentile 1975, p. 364; pp. 374–375).

Another aspect explored by Emilio Gentile was the "ideology of the leader", one of the distinctive and constituent elements of fascist ideology, elaborated by Mussolini himself. He constructed the myth of the *duce* on the model of the leader drawn by the French sociologist Gustave Le Bon, who had forecast that the twentieth century would be the "century of the crowds": crowds who had little inclination for rational thought, but were ready for action and in need of a leader who could understand their psychology—naturally conservative and tied to race and tradition (Gentile 1975, pp. 401–403).

Anticipating many recent studies on the cult of Mussolini, Isnenghi also included the cult as a feature of fascist ideology in his arguments about the construction of consensus. He analysed the regime's reports of the speeches Mussolini conducted in Italy's city squares (for example, by intellectuals such as Ugo Ojetti and Guido Piovene). They showed the coexistence of two notions of heroism: the "horizontal heroism" of the crowd, realised through anonymous discipline, the abnegation of the individual, and the virtue of obedience, and the "vertical heroism" of the *duce*, expressing the virtue of command (Isnenghi 1979 [2], p. 12). Isnenghi also underlined the existence of hundreds of biographies of Mussolini while he was alive (to which Luisa Passerini devoted her work *Mussolini immaginario* in 1991), as well as thousands of personal letters in which Italians asked for help and intercession, confided their problems, and found an outlet with the One who could understand everything: a process that lent Mussolini the status of a thaumaturge, or a popular saint (Isnenghi 1979 [2], pp. 16–17).

The First Studies on Fascist Colonialism

One of the major developments in the historiography of the 1960s and 1970s was the shift of focus to examine not just the regime in Italy but the operation of fascism in Italy's empire. In a book published in 1965 on the Abyssinian war (1935–1941), Angelo Del Boca provided the first serious account of fascist colonialism, using the Italian and Ethiopian documents available at the time. Through interviews with survivors, Italian army documents printed in Ethiopia and correspondence between Mussolini, marshal Pietro Badoglio and marshal Rodolfo Graziani, Del Boca demonstrated for the first time the substantial use of poison gas by the Italian air forces against the Ethiopian civilian population and army in order to quell their resistance (Del Boca 1965, pp. 73–77). This was an issue that De Felice had almost entirely ignored.

Del Boca continued to explore the subject in greater detail through to the 1990s, generating in the process an important public debate about the nature of fascist imperialism. Building on Del Boca's work, the first important general account on Italian colonialism, including its relationship with fascism, came in 1973 from the military historian Giorgio Rochat. He focused particularly on the Italian wars in East Africa and in Libya, and the way these territories were governed. Until then, the subject had been largely unexplored, except for a number of romanticised memoirs that often retained racist convictions and even influenced school textbooks of the time. Rochat highlighted stories that described "naive and ferocious savages, officers without fear and without reproach and heroic soldiers, to which it was obligatory to add a generic lamentation about the horrors of colonial wars, immediately corrected by a reference to the very Italian capacity to establish human contact with the African subjects" (Rochat 1973, p. 9).

To replace those imaginary reports with a historically-grounded reconstruction, Rochat analysed mainly official and fascist sources, the start of a long-term project that he shared with other colonial and military historians, and which expanded in the 1990s thanks to newly-opened archives. Although at the time it was difficult to precisely calculate the costs of the repression, Rochat demonstrated how the "reconquest" of Libya (as Giolitti's conquest of Libya in 1912 had remained limited to coastal areas), resulted in destruction of Libyan resistance by 1928–1930, and ended with the deportation, under Graziani's leadership, of the whole population of Gebel to concentration camps for two years and the destruction of their livestock. Rochat showed that according to Italian official estimates, Cyrenaica (eastern Libya) had some 225,000 inhabitants in the 1920s, while the census of 1931 recorded 142,000. Around 20,000 people escaped into Egypt, while 60,000 died of hunger or illness during the deportation (Rochat 1973, pp. 99–101).

His work on the conquest of Ethiopia he linked to Mussolini's foreign policy, explaining how the choice to invade was made in 1934 in response to the consequences of the 1929 financial crash, in an attempt to relaunch the Italian economy and confront the low morale of the population. The invasion represented a propaganda diversion as well as the possibility of economic recovery, given that Mussolini hoped Ethiopia would be full of raw material resources and good farming land. Acquiring new markets and raw material in Africa was an attractive policy also because British and French opposition was expected to be a formality, since both countries counted on Italy's support to contain German rearmament. For Mussolini, it had to be not simply a colonial, but a national war, with a huge military display, to engage the population through propaganda. Ultimately, the war appeared to be the solution to all problems and the conquest led to the highest point of the consensus for the regime among the Italian population (Rochat 1973, pp. 137–140).

Rochat also mentioned the use of poison gas, but could not yet provide more information than Del Boca had; however, based on an analysis of papers held in the National Archives in Rome—correspondence between political and military leaders, fascist directives, the press, the testimonies of Italian generals and laws applied to the colonies—he was able to reconstruct the politics of terror against the Ethiopian population and its resistance from the winter of 1936–1937. This included the torching of villages, the shooting of peasants, the massacre of livestock, and bombing, as well as racial discrimination and the achievement of the total obliteration of the Ethiopian ruling class (Rochat 1973, p. 183). In 1976 Rochat thoroughly criticised De Felice's fourth volume of Mussolini's biography, which dealt with the period of the conquest of Ethiopia, for its lack of interest in Mussolini's foreign and military policies, and in the aspects of repression and violence these policies entailed. The problem also existed, wrote Rochat in an article in *Italia Contemporanea*, in De Felice's previous volumes, where he overlooked the long war for the "reconquest" of Libya between 1922 and 1932. Rochat pointed to the existence of a wealth of documentation ignored by De Felice that demonstrated Mussolini's personal role in preparing wars of great ambition and scale, and their tragic consequences for the populations of Libya and Ethiopia (Rochat in *Italia Contemporanea* 1976, pp. 91–92).

Building on work by Rochat and Del Boca, historians later documented the connections between the history of Italian colonialism and that of fascist racism. But important steps in this direction were already evident in the 1960s, when De Felice's work on the Jews in Italy during fascism (De Felice 1961) suggested that the racist laws of 1938 were partly a result of the Rome-Berlin Axis alliance of 1936—not because there was interference from Germany, but as an opportunistic choice by Mussolini to gratify his ally. De Felice used the issue to clarify Italian legislative autonomy from Germany, while at the same time underlining the importance of German influence in general terms. These were arguments that De Felice returned to in the fifth volume of Mussolini's biography published in 1981, and they were immediately criticised by Rochat. In a review of the volume, Rochat disputed the idea that Mussolini was practically obliged to pursue a racist policy by the German alliance, or that he applied it mildly: De Felice had chosen his documents partially, relying mostly on fascist sources, and ignored the practical consequences of the racist laws of 1938 as well as the ruthless racism and atrocities unleashed against the Ethiopian population, which ended only with Italy's defeat in the African war (Rochat in *Italia Contemporanea* 1981, pp. 5–6; 8).

THE CONTROVERSIES IN THE 1970S AND 1980S

Rochat's criticism of De Felice has turned out to be well-grounded. A wealth of new research from the 1990s onwards has demonstrated that many of De Felice's interpretations have not stood the test of time. However, in the 1970s and the 1980s the debate on the interpretation of fascism was still grounded in the issues raised by De Felice's work. In the first place, his methodology was contested: he mostly referred to fascist sources and built his biography around a reconstruction of what appeared to have been Mussolini's intentions, at the expense of the actual results of his policies. But increasingly, the principal accusation concerned De Felice's political agenda: a former communist when he was a university student in Rome, he turned anti-communist and from then on tried to delegitimise anti-fascism. By presenting fascism as a benevolent regime, different in both origin and practice from German Nazism, not really totalitarian in character, and partly based on mass consensus, he drew the conclusion that anti-fascism was no longer meaningful or valuable. In the 1980s his interpretations were simplified by the media, which presented him as a reasonable historian who was finally challenging the left-wing predominance that had prevailed in Italian culture since 1945.

Tommaso Baris and Alessio Gagliardi have recently contextualised this controversy, explaining the polemical excesses it generated partly as a result of the climate of political instability of the country. After the neo-fascist atrocities of the 1970s (starting with a bomb in Piazza Fontana in Milan in 1969 that killed 16 people) and the military coup in Chile in 1973, a section of public opinion, including intellectuals and historians, began to fear the possibility of a military authoritarian takeover in Italy. The attempt by the media to draw on De Felice's work in order to downplay the role of anti-fascism in the Italian Republic, and to present an indulgent attitude towards the fascist regime, was part of a wider attempt to delegitimise the left, whether socialist, communist, or social-catholic. New accounts of fascism appeared in the 1980s, written chiefly by journalists who relied on De Felice rather than undertaking historical research on their own behalf (for example Arrigo Petacco, Antonio Spinosa and Giordano Bruno Guerri). These were histories of fascism based on the private life of Mussolini and other fascist leaders, often characterised by a nostalgic tone, abandoning any critical judgment on the regime and, in effect, rehabilitating fascism. This revisionism set the tone for a great many television series and magazines that reached the wider public. It proved to be a difficult situation for historians to confront. Nicola Tranfaglia proposed the need for a historiographical revival, blaming anti-fascist historical writing for having insisted on a "celebratory anti-fascism" that was too moralistic and rhetorical (Baris and Gagliardi in *Studi Storici* 2014, pp. 322–328). A lively and critical response to this question and the themes that it raised developed from the 1990s onwards.

Despite the controversies, important bases were built in the four decades after the end of the war for a study of fascism that went beyond the question of its origins to focus on the fascist regime in power, raising issues that have continued to be discussed up to the present day. The questions of consensus, totalitarianism, the construction of the dictatorship, fascist culture and ideology, and fascist militarism and colonialism were re-evaluated and revised by a new historiography that developed a fruitful and critical relationship with the research and interpretations produced between the 1960s and the 1980s.

References

Aquarone, Alberto, *L'organizzazione dello Stato totalitario* (Turin: Einaudi, 1965).
Arendt, Hannah, *Le origini del totalitarismo* (Turin: Einaudi, 2021; 1st ed. New York 1951; first Italian ed. 1967).
Baldoli, Claudia, *Bissolati immaginario. Le origini dle fascismo cremonese. Dal socialismo riformista allo squadrismo* (Cremona: cremonabooks, 2002).

Banfi, Antonio, *Studio sulle origini e la natura del fascismo*, in *Saggi sul marxismo* (Rome: Editori Riuniti, 1960).

Chabod, Federico, *L'Italia contemporanea* (Turin: Einaudi, 1961).

Chessa, Pasquale, Villari, Francesco *Interpretazioni su Renzo De Felice* (Milan: Baldini & Castoldi 2002).

Cuzzi, Marco, Dondi, Mirco, Guzzo, Domenico, *La strategia della tensione tra piazza Fontana e l'Italicus. Fenomenologia, rappresentazioni, memoria* (Milan: Biblion, 2022).

De Felice, Renzo, *Storia degli ebrei italiani sotto il fascismo* (Turin: Einaudi, 1961).

De Felice, Renzo, *Mussolini il rivoluzionario, 1883–1920* (Turin: Einaudi, 1965).

De Felice, Renzo, *Mussolini il fascista*, vol. 1, *La conquista del potere* (Turin: Einaudi, 1966).

De Felice, Renzo, *Mussolini il fascista*, vol. 2, *L'organizzazione dello Stato fascista* (Turin: Einaudi, 1968).

De Felice, Renzo, *Le interpretazioni del fascismo* (Bari: Laterza, 1969).

De Felice, Renzo, *Mussolini il duce*, vol. 1, *Gli anni del consenso, 1929–1936* (Turin: Einaudi, 1974).

De Felice, Renzo, *Intervista sul fascismo*, ed. by Michael Ledeen (Rome-Bari: Laterza, 1975).

De Felice, Renzo, *Mussolini il duce*, vol. 2, *Lo Stato totalitario, 1936–1940* (Turin: Einaudi, 1981).

Del Boca, Angelo, *La guerra d'Abissinia, 1935-1941* (Milan: Feltrinelli, 1965).

Del Noce, Augusto, *Fascismo e antifascismo. Errori della cultura* (Milan: Mondadori, 1995).

De Rosa, Gabriele *Storia del Partito Popolare* (Bari: Laterza, 1958).

Franzinelli, Mimmo, *Squadristi. Protagonisti e tecniche della violenza fascista, 1919–1922* (Milan: Mondadori, 2003).

Franzinelli, Mimmo, *Fascismo anno zero. 1919: la nascita dei fasci italiani di combattimento* (Milan: Mondadori, 2019).

Gentile, Emilio, *Le origini dell'ideologia fascista (1918–1925)* (Rome-Bari: Laterza, 1975).

Gentile, Emilio, *La via italiana al totalitarismo. Il partito e lo Stato nel regime fascista* Rome: La Nuova Italia Scientifica, 1995).

Isnenghi, Mario, *Intellettuali militanti e intellettuali funzionari* (Turin: Einaudi, 1979 [1]) .

Isnenghi, Mario, *L'Educazione dell'italiano. Il fascismo e l'organizzazione della cultura* (Bologna: Cappelli, 1979 [2]).

Lyttelton, Adrian, *La conquista del potere* (Rome-Bari: Laterza, 1974).

Mangoni, Luisa, *L'interventismo della cultura. Intellettuali e riviste del fascismo* (Rome-Bari: Laterza, 1974).

Nenni, Pietro, *Storia di quattro anni, 1919–1922. La crisi socialista dal 1919 al 1922* (Milan: Libreria del Quarto Stato, 1926).

Palla, Marco, "La conquista fascista del potere", in *Studi Storici*, n. 4, 1974, pp. 968–984.

Procacci, Giuliano, *Storia degli italiani* (Bari: Laterza, 1968).

Quazza, Guido (ed.), *Fascismo e società italiana* (Turin: Einaudi, 1973).

Rochat, Giorgio, *Il colonialismo italiano* (Turin: Loescher, 1973).

Rochat, Giorgio, "Il quarto volume della biografia di Mussolini di Renzo De Felice", in *Italia Contemporanea*, n. 118, 1976, pp. 89–102.

Rochat, Giorgio, "Ancora sul 'Mussolini' di Renzo De Felice", in *Italia Contemporanea*, n. 144, 1981, pp. 5–10.
Salvemini, Gaetano, *Le origini del fascismo in Italia. Lezioni di Harvard* (Milan: Feltrinelli, 1966).
Sapelli, Giulio, *Introduzione*, in Fondazione Feltrinelli, *Annali*, n. 20, 1979–1980, *La classe operaia durante il fascismo* (Milan: Feltrinelli, 1981).
Scoppola, Pietro, La Chiesa e il fascismo: documenti e interpretazioni (Bari: Laterza, 1976).
Scoppola, Pietro, Traniello, Francesco, *I cattolici tra fascismo e democrazia* (Bologna: Il Mulino, 1975).
Studi Storici, special issue: "Fascismo: Itinerari storiografici da un secolo all'altro", n. 1, 2014.
Sturzo, Luigi, *Il Partito popolare italiano* (Bologna: Zanichelli, 1957).
Tasca, Angelo, *Nascita e avvento del fascismo* (Bari: Laterza, 1965; first ed., Paris 1938; first Italian ed. Florence: La Nuova Italia, 1950; English ed. 2010).
Turati, Filippo, *Ciò che l'Italia insegna. Per un'unica internazionale dei lavoratori del mondo* (Milan: Critica Sociale, 1945).
Valeri, Nino, *Da Giolitti a Mussolini. Momenti della crisi del liberalismo* (Florence: Parenti, 1956).

CHAPTER 4

The Historiography of Fascism from the End of the Cold War

The fall of the Berlin wall in November 1989 symbolised the end of the Cold War, indicating the imminent disaggregation of the communist empire, which had embodied for decades the myth of communism in the eyes of millions of the "faithful" (Colarizi 2007, p. 172). This political earthquake also had an impact in Italy, the only western country where the communist party (PCI) carried important weight in national politics (even though it was always in opposition and never in government) and was still the second political force in 1989. The collapse of the Soviet Union came at the same time as Europe was preparing for the Maastricht treaty of 1992, which in Italy meant that questions of huge public debt and political corruption were surfacing. With the end of communism, the age of totalitarianism seemed a closed chapter in the history of Europe. In Italy, meagre results for the neo-fascist party MSI in the 1990 national elections led to a new course the following year when the leader, Gianfranco Fini, undertook its transition to a post-fascist party. In the meantime, the leader of the PCI, Achille Occhetto, led the party into a post-communist phase, renaming it the Democratic Party of the Left (PDS), amidst the protest of a minority who still saw themselves as communist and established the *Rifondazione Comunista* party [Communist re-foundation] to continue the experience.

These were also years when the main parties of government, the Christian democrats (DC) and the socialist party (PSI), began to be implicated in corruption scandals, as independent judges uncovered a system of the illegal exchange of favours and votes between politicians and the business world—and in some cases the Mafia. This general delegitimization of political parties proved advantageous to the Northern League, a new party that represented the rich regions of the north at the time of European integration. The League presented itself as anti-ideological and posed questions that many Italians in everyday life could relate to: its attack on the parties reflected the evident inefficiency of public structures, as well as the corruption within them; the alleged costs of

© The Author(s), under exclusive license to Springer Nature
Switzerland AG 2023
C. Baldoli, *Italian Fascism, 1914-1945*,
https://doi.org/10.1007/978-3-031-41904-1_4

supporting an unproductive south; and the difficulty involved in integrating foreign workers (Colarizi 2007, p. 193). With the "clean hands" operation led by magistrates in Milan—also called *Tangentopoli* (kick-back city)—a whole ruling class was put on trial in 1992. Only the parties that had not been in government during the post-war decades survived: the PDS, the League, and the MSI. Indeed, Fini supported the judges in order to promote the image of the MSI as an uncorrupted party that had always been at the margins of the system. The fascist stigma, however, remained a problem, which he resolved in 1994 by changing the identity of the party, now named the National Alliance (AN). The party officially detached itself from fascism, condemning Nazi-fascist crimes and the racist laws of 1938. Silvio Berlusconi, founder of a private television empire built also on political support from the leader of the PSI, Bettino Craxi, established another political party, Forza Italia. Berlusconi presented himself as the personally charismatic bearer of a business culture, who could fill the void left by the crisis of the traditional parties, and build a political force that could stop the left gaining power, since the PDS was the only large party remaining from the old system. A successful man for a TV audience of millions, he also received votes from former DC and PSI supporters.

History became a "very political battleground" in the media during this period (Colarizi 2007, p. 221). The idea purported by AN, which entered government in 1994 in alliance with Berlusconi's party and the League, was that anti-fascism as well as fascism must be left in the past. This argument was rejected by the left, which showed how difficult it was to find new identities. In recent works, historians have explained the AN's identity as "suspended" between nostalgia for the fascist past and the various exhortations of its leaders for the renewal of its political culture (Ridolfi 2008, p. 216). Indeed, its adhesion to liberal democracy while maintaining its roots in the RSI has been underlined (Ignazi 2018, pp. 121–122).

According to historian Sergio Luzzatto, the turning point in the discussion on fascism was not 1994, but 1989: nowhere in Europe, including Italy, had anti-fascism been uncoupled from communism, so with the latter's defeat, anti-fascism was also discredited (Luzzatto 2004, p. 8). In Isnenghi's view, this was partly provoked by the PCI itself, because of its inability to confront its own past: the party wrecked half a century of history all at once, by rejecting the image that had been constructed by its opponents—that of the "party of Moscow"—without emphasising that it had actually been a mass party that took an active role in democratic politics (Isnenghi 2011a, b, p. 639).

This political turmoil had important consequences for the development of the historiography on both fascism and anti-fascism. The 1990s saw the emergence of studies by a new generation of history students, a cohort that developed intellectually after the fall of the Soviet Union and which shared the sense of disorientation caused not only by the redesigning of geographical borders, but especially by the collapse of a whole hierarchy of cultural meanings, ways of life and countless individual biographies (Snodi 2007, p. x). The end of the ideological polarisation between capitalism and communism led to a study of fascism that was freer than that of preceding decades. This new body of historians does not seem to have created academic "schools" or to have taken a particular ideological line, a fact evident in the creation of new historical journals in print and online, and the changing composition of established editorial boards. On the contrary, many of the recent works on fascism suggest a conscious will on their part to distance themselves from the idea of linking political belonging and historical research.

In the post-1989 context, the media found De Felice's historiography to be particularly pertinent. Some of his interpretations became once again sources of controversy, for example the negation of a general theory of fascism in order to overlook the movement's international dimension; or his definition of the anti-fascist Resistance of 1943–1945 as a minority movement, with the aim of diminishing the role of anti-fascism and the Resistance in Italy's post-war history. With his eight-volume biography of Mussolini, De Felice's work no doubt represents an indispensable documentary contribution, providing interpretations and hypotheses that have stimulated important debates. However, he lost prestige as a historian, particularly from the end of the 1980s, by abandoning scholarly work in order to make unfounded claims in the media that served to rehabilitate fascism and devalue the significance of the Resistance and the post-war constitution (Santomassimo in *Italia Contemporanea* 1998, p. 556). The following were the aspects of De Felice's historiography that continued to raise controversy: an interpretation of the passivity of the masses as evidence of consensus for the regime, which initiated an ongoing debate that still informs recent studies; little interest in Mussolini's brutal repression of the Libyan resistance and in Ethiopia, and, in general, a reconstruction of fascist foreign and colonial policy that attenuated its aggressive connotations; the underestimation of the role of the Italian Social Republic (RSI, 1943–1945) in the Holocaust, with the consequent denial of Italian fascism's direct responsibility in the extermination of the Jews; and finally, that fascism was not a totalitarian system, in comparison with the Soviet Union and Nazi Germany. In sum, De Felice's revisionist views of the regime, endorsed by his role in the popular media, provoked a long-running argument with historians whose views were broadly anti-fascist.

Contrary to De Felice's denial of the existence of a European fascist phenomenon, recent historiography has begun stimulating research, revealing the transnational nature of fascism and promoting fruitful comparisons between fascisms in different countries. De Felice's conviction of the ideological difference between fascism and Nazism, thanks to the support of the Italian media, has meant a different approach to the theme of Italian anti-Semitism in comparison with German racism, while his attribution of benevolent features to Italian fascism has deliberately distanced the Italian experience from the German. On both themes recent historiography has entirely revised De Felice's interpretations, which have proved to be weak from the point of view of methodology and analysis, but which have nonetheless enjoyed great success at the level of public opinion. The same is true for his treatment of foreign policy throughout the Mussolini biography, which is now mostly rejected by historians. De Felice's Mussolini is a character continuously forced by circumstances to make choices that contrasted with his real inclinations: he did not want a war in Ethiopia but rather a pacific annexation, he would have preferred not to enter the Spanish Civil War or the alliance with Germany, and, in fact, would have preferred to find agreement with Britain in order to restrain Hitler. The idea that emerges is of a distance between Mussolini and Nazism precisely at the point when the two regimes moved into closer alliance. De Felice's biographical work largely concentrates on the temperament and the personality of the subject, rather than on his concrete acts; with this approach the outcome of the Second World War, for example, appears accidental rather than the result of political choices taken by Mussolini in the years beforehand.

Given the political context of the 1990s, the debate took the shape of "revisionism" against "anti-revisionism", "*defeliciani*" against "anti-*defeliciani*". History began to look like a besieged citadel to be defended from media attacks. As we shall see, the latest historiography has reached a point when it is possible to consider De Felice's work with more detachment, thanks to the wealth of research and interpretation that the present generation of historians has produced.

NEW RESEARCH ON THE ORIGINS OF FASCISM

War, Post-war and Political Violence

Fascism is no longer studied only as a phenomenon of class reaction, or as a rejection of modernity in favour of tradition, but as a political, social, and cultural movement that inserted itself into the political and social processes that began in Europe with the French revolution, continued in the conflicts and tensions of mass modernity, and accelerated violently during the social mobilisation produced in European society by the First World War. The new historiography has confirmed the view of the First World War as the real matrix of fascism, although other pre-existing political traditions were influential, such as the myths and lay rituals of nineteenth century mass movements, or the neo-romanticism, irrationalism, activism, and anti-parliamentarianism of the new radical anti-liberal movements that emerged in Europe and in Italy by the beginning of the war (Gentile 2002, p. 45).

Fundamental to reflections on the relationship between fascism and political violence are the works of Emilio Gentile and George Mosse (1990). Their research demonstrated how the experience of war—violence and death, habituation to indifference for human life—contributed to the decision of many ex-servicemen to join the fascist squads and provided a fertile terrain for the development of fascism (Albanese in *Studi Storici* 2014, p. 4). They proposed an analysis of the long-term effects of the brutalisation of politics, even at times independent from political motivation.

Even more than anti-Bolshevik, fascist violence was focused against liberal democracy, as evidenced by studies on the fascist takeover of the provinces, which demonstrated how the results of free democratic elections were subverted with violence. This hatred of democracy was the basis of the choice made to belong to a squad, which demonstrates a certain level of consensus to fascism even *before* the regime came to power; it was a voluntary act, and thus a more authentic consensus than the one claimed to exist during the dictatorship (Millan in Albanese 2021, p. 31).

Studies on the role of violence and the brutalisation of politics in the first post-war years have drawn on research not only in (and on) Italy—such as those by Eric Leed (1979) and Antonio Gibelli (1991)—which has shown how the experience of war was one of the bases for supporting fascism. Historians have also investigated the roots of fascist violence in early twentieth-century culture. As Angelo Ventrone has argued, the age of nationalism launched the idea of the "ethic of war"—the war experience implied a duty to regenerate a decaying society. He observed that it is difficult for us now to understand sentiments so different from the later twentieth century that exalted war, violence, and sacrifice and accepted the dominant role of the elite. This lack of empathy has made it difficult to interpret the fascist regime, whose ideology was seen as simply based on propaganda, manipulation, and a thirst for power, rather than being centred on the idea of the regenerating capacity of struggle and war (Ventrone 2003, p. 67). Gentile, too, in a book first published in 1982 and revisited in 1999, analysed the cultural ground that predated fascism as an ideology. He argued that the connection between fascism and pre-war radical nationalism does not mean endorsing the argument that radical nationalism was a form of "proto-fascism" or a form of "fascism before fascism". Within radical nationalist ideology there also existed ideas of cultural and political freedom, the emancipation of the masses, the defence of individual autonomy: all these prevailed over the ideas that favoured authoritarian solutions. Moreover, argued Gentile, the culture of radical nationalism that shaped the views of politicians and intellectuals opposed to Giolittian liberalism, produced both future fascists and anti-fascists. The fascist myth of the "new state" was instead a result of the Great War, *squadrismo* and the fascist party rather than the age of Giolitti; but at the same time, understanding the ideas of radical nationalism is fundamental for an understanding of fascism (Gentile 1999, p. xiii).

As well as the work of Gentile, Isnenghi's research has continued to be influential in understanding the origins of fascism. Reflecting on his earlier studies, he returned in 2008 to evaluate the significance of early-century periodicals, not only those linked to the Neapolitan philosophers who gathered around Croce's *La Critica*, but also linked to Giovanni Gentile, and the young literati in Florence, who focused on signalling their distance from the older generation—that is, from Risorgimento patriotism, the Mazzinian idea of the nation, and socialism. Corradini's *Il Regno* supported a new form of nationalism, expansionistic and warrior-like, which also influenced Papini's *Leonardo*. The pre-war, and later interventionist, generation of intellectuals wrote in

Prezzolini's *La Voce*; but so too did a liberal (and, later, leading anti-fascist) like Giovanni Amendola, who proclaimed: "We dislike Italy as it is now"; and Mussolini, who signed his articles *Homme qui cherche*—that is, both future fascists and future anti-fascists. Salvemini opposed the Libyan war and left *La Voce* to found *L'Unità*; Marinetti founded the futurist *Poesia*; in 1913 Papini and Ardengo Soffici created *Lacerba*, the most aggressive newspaper at the service of interventionism in 1914. As a way out of the crisis, some of these dissatisfied intellectuals indicated war as an existential and social remedy (Isnenghi in Isnenghi and Ceschin 2008, p. 106).

The interventionist campaign produced suspicion, discontent, and hatred. Private citizens declared themselves to be above the civil authorities. The deep transformations produced by the war showed the inadequacies of the "old" political rules of the liberal state and promoted new ones: the pre-eminence of patriotic values, which for many became the only criterion for judging actions and choices; the appropriation of these values by ordinary people who intended to conquer the state as the only representatives of the "real" national interest; the attempt to silence any dissenting voice; the systematic use of violence and its justification; the will to unify the struggle against external and internal enemies; and finally new definitions of *italianità*, or national culture. A few years later these elements all became ingredients of the fascist political project, but were first defined during the First World War. As a result, Ventrone has argued, it is necessary to retrospectively date many of the "novelties" introduced into Italian politics by fascism (Ventrone 2003, pp. vii–xi). One example is provided by forms of violence: during interventionist meetings Austrian flags and images or puppets of the emperor appeared, to be burned publicly as with traditional forms of popular protest. There was also the imposition on local orchestras to play national anthems, or on hotels to display the tricolour flag; there were night-time attacks on German shops or companies, and assaults on socialist headquarters. These all marked a new direction in the nature of Italian political conflict (Ventrone 2003, p. 69).

The image of the liberal state as it was perceived by its contemporaries, especially in political culture, was generally negative, although subsequent historical research has demonstrated the progress achieved from the time of unification. But the contemporary images obscured the positive aspects and influenced the behaviour and beliefs of the new generation. One influence derived from the accusation made by the nineteenth-century nationalist Mazzini that the Risorgimento, with its liberal-monarchic outcome, was an incomplete revolution. Mazzini's thought was not systematically analysed by early twentieth-century nationalists, and he was clearly not a precursor of fascism. Nevertheless, there is some common ground between his view of the nation and the later anti-socialist and anti-democratic ideological strands. Nationalism, with its dissatisfied need for the grandeur of the Italian state, could be seen as a "modern variant of Mazzinian Italianism" (Gentile 1999, pp. 5–9). Simon Levis Sullam has shown that Mussolini, in his turn to interventionism, found himself immersed in a patriotic atmosphere in which there were recurring references to

Mazzini. He has concluded that Mazzini would probably have followed the same path from social revolution to national revolution followed by Mussolini (Levis Sullam 2010, p. 58).

The radicalisation of the interventionist-neutralist divide took place after Caporetto, between 1917 and 1919. Isnenghi has identified two processes at work during that period. While officers and intellectuals continued to support the reassuring idea of a patient peasant-people as an instrument of the state's will, the reality of the situation imposed itself, overturning their ideological fantasy: the revolts for peace and bread in Turin in August 1917, and the defeat at Caporetto in October, both changed dramatically the face of the war. The blame for the defeat was initially placed on the soldiers by their commander, General Luigi Cadorna, but was quickly transferred to the "political instigators" within the country, even though the actual responsibility for the defeat lay with the military leadership (Isnenghi 2007, pp. 333–335). A majority of democratic and revolutionary interventionists came to believe that war was an opportunity to establish a new moral discipline for Italians, and to gradually abandon—temporarily for some, definitively for others—their own original ideals.

The idea that the war would eliminate the Austrian empire and even the monarchy in Italy also motivated a number of revolutionaries (Mussolini among them) to abandon their previous position and to support a war between nations which Marxist doctrine had identified as the main expression of the bourgeois oppression of the working class (Ventrone 2003, pp. 29–34). Futurism also made an important contribution. Despite some superficial contact with the Milanese socialists, its founder Marinetti was opposed to socialism as both an idea and a political movement. At the root of his anti-socialism was his exasperated patriotism, his aversion to pacifism, and his hostility to a society organised along principles of equality. In Marinetti's view, it was possible to combine the revolutionary aspirations of the proletariat with nationalism and the futurist exaltation of war (Gentile 1999, pp. 143–146). Indeed, the futurist groups were the basis of the March 1919 constitution of the *fasci*. Their objectives were the defence of interventionism, the fight against socialism, the abolition of the monarchy, and the idea that combatants had the right to direct the transformation of the political regime. As Giulia Albanese has argued, plans were developed among these groups for direct action and coups, some for an internal revolution in Italy and others for Italian control over Dalmatia (Albanese 2006, p. 6).

In a work that reflected on the centenary of the march on Rome in 2022, building on previous research by Albanese, Mimmo Franzinelli reiterated the importance of recognising the thuggish elements in early fascism: the readiness to employ physical violence expressed the essence of the spirit of 1919, which was not content with the defeat of political enemies but wanted to humiliate and mortify them. One example of this spirit was the fascist Ferruccio Vecchi, a war misfit, ready for any violence and incapable of adapting to civilian life; another was the destruction and looting of the offices of the socialist newspaper *Avanti!* in April 1919 in Milan, after which the fascists took gadgets and objects they had stolen from the newsroom to the headquarters of *Il Popolo d'Italia*, as trophies (Franzinelli 2022, p. 13; p. 23). Acts of violence that, according to Marco Mondini, were products of the manichean logic of war, which had persuaded the fascists they had the right and the duty to seize power in order to redeem the nation and transform the Italians, even at the cost of exterminating anyone who did not agree with them. The war would not end until that mission was accomplished (Mondini 2022, p. 14).

Studies on the origins of fascism have also engaged with the historiography on Fiume, particularly lively around the centenary of its occupation by D'Annunzio in 2019. Among others, Federico Carlo Simonelli has emphasised the legacy of the ritual and symbolic aspects of D'Annunzio's enterprise for fascist public narrative and the use of public space under the regime. These included the cult of the leader, the myth of voluntarism, the cult of youth and virility, of body and sport, the cult of death, of violence, blood, and martyrs, with simulated battles and spectacles designed to demonstrate that D'Annunzio's followers were real combatants ready to return to the trenches (Simonelli 2021, p. 243). Many military personnel took part in the invasion of Fiume, in other words the very people who should instead have suppressed attempts at subversion (Albanese 2006, p. 8). As Isenghi has argued, D'Annunzio drew on national ideological traditions, from ancient Rome to the maritime republics, to the Savoy monarchy and Garibaldi: a whole classical repertoire was mobilised to support the message of just and sacred war, in which the citizen's role was one of devotion and submission (Isnenghi 2007, p. 107). As Milza underlined in his 2000 biography of Mussolini, the latter took from the Fiume adventure not only the rituals developed by D'Annunzio, the dialogues with the crowds, the black uniform symbolising death, the war rhetoric, but also some political lessons: the weakness of the state and the complicity that could be found among some of its representatives, the attraction among the masses for a political formula that could unite national sentiment and social claims, the need to create a disciplined and structured political organisation. The failure of Fiume thus left the field free for fascism (Milza 2000, p. 287).

Historians have also engaged with earlier arguments about the crisis of the liberal state in the face of social crisis, a perspective that has been explored in a three-volume study of the origins of fascism by Roberto Vivarelli. Based on a vast range of archival sources, Vivarelli has argued that the success of the fascist movement was "the fruit and not the cause" of the crisis of the liberal state, providing a wealth of detail on what could be defined as a one-way civil war in 1919–1922 (Vivarelli 1991, vol. 2, p. 7). In dialogue with his conclusions, studies appeared in the 2000s that explored the relationship between fascist violence, social unrest, and the strike movement, intertwining local and national history (Albanese 2006; Fincardi 2008). By 1921 it had become clear, even to those who had been opportunist about fascism, that the latter was not simply an anti-Bolshevik reaction but a movement against any liberal institution, against freedom of expression and individual rights. The continual planning for coups within the nationalist and military environments and the repetition of anti-liberal and anti-parliamentarian discourses and perspectives demonstrated, as Albanese has argued, the progressive coagulation and strengthening of groups whose aim it was to overrule the parliamentary system and exclude from politics not only the socialists, but also the section of the ruling class that wanted a progressive democratisation of the liberal state (Albanese 2006, p. 18).

As Matteo Di Figlia explained in a biography of one of the most radical fascist leaders, Farinacci, the acts of extreme violence that ended in the murder of socialist or catholic leaders at times managed to spread panic and disorientation among anti-fascists, while emboldening the fascists, who rather than denying, boasted about carrying out beatings and homicides (Di Figlia 2007, pp. 61–62). Not only had the fascists inherited the will to occupy public space from the interventionists of 1915 (they were, after all, in many cases the same people), but they also had more weapons at their disposal and were more prepared for combat (Albanese 2006, p. 19). For many squad leaders, the aim of the violence was to restore social order, but for many others, *squadrismo* was the experience of a "totalitarian community" that came from the trenches. Squad participants were united by a cause—complicity in violent action, the religious idea of the nation, and the cult of the fallen both in the war and in the post-war violence. The enemies had to be physically eliminated or reduced to passive obedience. Local leaders were acclaimed by their followers; this armed militia had rituals and symbols and, according to Gentile, anticipated the totalitarian nature of fascism (Gentile 1999, pp. 29–30).

Following the long-term trajectory of fascist violence, it is possible to find common ground between the most violent fascists and Mussolini even after the march on Rome. The fascist laws against freedom of the press, the institution of internal exile and the Special Tribunal for State Security illustrated that the murder of Matteotti was not an accident within a law-abiding process of affirmation for fascism, but was one of the steps undertaken by fascism in the construction of the dictatorship. The regime's (and Mussolini's) direct responsibility in it was precisely demonstrated for the first time by Mauro Canali in 1997. Moreover, violence was also used abroad, starting with the "reconquest" of Libya in the second half of the 1920s. Here was a continuation of *squadrismo*, expressed through the willingness to physically eliminate the enemy as racially different—a process that continued in the following decade in Ethiopia, Spain, and the Balkans. Violence was also employed for symbolic and psychological effect, even when it was not lethal. Hitting opponents with clubs, forcing them to drink castor oil, threatening castration, and sexual violence, were all intended to humiliate the victim and affirm the perpetrator's masculinity, a form of daily cruelty intended to intimidate that continued throughout the dictatorship (Millan in Albanese 2021, pp. 36–37).

Beyond Violence: What was the First Fascism?

The success of fascism, however, cannot be entirely explained through its violent politics. In defining fascism as a specific form of totalitarianism, Gentile argued that fascism was also born of an autonomous political impulse, developed according to its own logic and initiatives that were central to the conquest of power, the transformation of the regime and the construction of the totalitarian state. It was therefore a new phenomenon in European history, not simply a derivation from other phenomena such as class reaction or the vices of the Italian character, all views endorsed by the "classical" interpretations of fascism. The fascist party was characterised by a new elitist conception of politics, the expression of an active minority that destroyed the liberal regime and gave life to a totalitarian state, a collective experiment of regeneration imposed on Italians under the auspices of the single party (Gentile 1999, pp. xvi–xvii).

Fascism and futurism were the ingredients of a movement against the internal enemy and whoever dishonoured the sacrifices of war or criticised Italy's claims on its eastern borders. Mussolini wanted to change the social system and install a new type of state, rooted in the masses but at the same time valuing modern industrialists. He eventually overcame the divisions within the movement, grouping together revolutionaries and reactionaries, republicans, and monarchists, syndicalists and entrepreneurs. The meeting in San Sepolcro square in Milan in March 1919 was later sanctified by the regime as the birth of fascism, though anti-fascists had not seen it as such. Mussolini often referred to the founding moment, even in 1940 when Italy entered the war, in order to support the myth of the original revolutionary impulse. It remained a complex, contradictory, and ambiguous page in history. Members and sympathisers of the *fasci* included, for example, futurists, republicans such as Nenni, professors and university students, revolutionary syndicalists, ex-servicemen such as Ernesto Rossi, the jurist Silvio Trentin, among them people who later became enemies of the regime and were punished with prison, internal confinement or exile. Their presence in the first *fasci* shows the fluidity of early fascism (Franzinelli 2019, pp. 4–7; Ventura 2021, pp. 75–81). An important reference point here is the historiography on the origins of fascism (for example, Zeev Sternhell 1989) that focused on the permeability between right-wing nationalism and the anti-Marxist left (such as Sorel's revision of Marxism in France) that characterised European political life between end of the nineteenth century and the Second World War.

Another question raised by recent historiography concerns the geographical origins of fascism. The fact that fascism was born in Milan poses the question of the city's importance for Mussolini's movement (Granata 2018). In August 1921 the future *duce* remarked in an article in *Il Popolo d'Italia* that Milan had been the cradle of fascism: for at least a year fascism was based in Milan, at the time when the word fascism was totally ignored in the Po valley. However, even in Milan, the headquarters of *Il Popolo d'Italia* was like a citadel in enemy territory, where the majority of the population rejected the newspaper's national-patriotic stance (Franzinelli 2019, pp. 9–13). Franzinelli reconstructed the sources of funding that allowed the movement to continue despite the adverse conditions, and showed how Milanese entrepreneurs financed fascism from the start. Contributions came from city banks, industrialists, and company directors. The meeting at San Sepolcro took place in a city centre meeting room owned by an association of industrialist, agrarian and commercial interests, offered by a financier who had been sponsoring Mussolini for about five years (Franzinelli 2019, p. 25; p. 53). Mussolini had been capable in 1914 of getting funding for his newspaper from financiers, some industrial trusts and banks (as well as, secretly, the French government, which was interested in winning Italy to the side of the Entente). Many industrialists and financiers who had enriched themselves during the war supported the first *fasci*. Indeed, *Il Popolo d'Italia* carried two to three pages of advertising every day, pages that show the early support for Mussolini from the industrial world, especially heavy industry. Mussolini's election campaign too was financed by industrialists. Historiography has long debated whether the first fascism was an expression of the ambitions and anxieties of the petit bourgeoisie; from its funders it is clear that the political movement was instead supported by the most modern forces of capitalism (Franzinelli 2019, pp. 68–77).

After the election defeat, fascism began to change trajectory, as confirmed at the national congress in Milan in May 1920, which abandoned the programme of 1919 and turned to the right, now presenting itself as the political organisation of the productive bourgeoisie and the middle classes, groups that no longer felt represented by the traditional parties and the liberal state. The strengthening of *squadrismo* was particularly evident after the outcome of the autumn 1920 local elections, which resulted in a significant victory for the socialists. The fascist movement grew rapidly after 1920: membership increased from 20,165 in December 1920 to 187,588 in May 1921, surpassing 200,000 two months later. This new fascism was very different to that of 1919: it was an aggregation of the various provincial fascisms, concentrated in the rural areas of the Po valley and Tuscany, with little presence in the south except for a few areas of Apulia and Sicily, and was supported by the agrarian bourgeoisie. While condemning bourgeois society as materialistic and individualistic, the *fasci* positioned themselves as defenders of private property, exalting the bourgeoisie's ruling function and capitalism's historical role, calling for class collaboration to intensify productivity and a foreign policy directed towards power and expansion.

Recent historiography has thus confirmed arguments about the origins of fascism that had been advanced, with less documentary evidence, by some of the classical interpretations: the ideological commingling that derived from the war and the heterogeneity of the 1919 fascist programme have been revealed, and the support fascism received from the propertied class has been confirmed by both local and national studies. 1919 fascism has again been defined as a new "anti-party" that prepared for civil war in order to achieve power (Ventura 2021, p. 83).

Reassessing Mussolini

Historians have long focused on the shift in Mussolini's politics in 1914, when he turned to interventionism and was expelled by the socialist party, as the most significant moment in understanding his future political trajectory. But it has become important, in explaining that shift, to move beyond the contemporary accusations of opportunism on Mussolini's part to examine his ideology and cultural origins. As with fascism in general, historians have begun to investigate Mussolini's writing, speeches and actions more seriously. In this way, it has proved possible to locate the origins of Mussolini's nationalism and anti-socialism in the years before 1914. Also from this point of view, recent writing has gone beyond De Felice's idea of a revolutionary Mussolini until 1920.

Historians have analysed Mussolini's views when he was a reader of *La Voce* and recognised his intellectual debt to the anti-Giolittian intellectual Prezzolini. At the time (1909) Mussolini was an internationalist and defined patriotism as an invention for defending the interests of the bourgeoisie. However, he did recognise the feeling for the *patria*, as a sense of belonging to an ethnic, cultural, and linguistic community that could not be ignored by the workers' movement, and shared the discontent of *La Voce* with contemporary Italy. On the other hand, Prezzolini and *La Voce* appreciated Mussolini, if not the socialist party, and applauded, for example, the "red week" (a mass agitation that spread all over Italy in June 1914) as a revolutionary moment that highlighted the divisions in the country, in particular those between the people and the ruling class (Gentile 1999, pp. 113–126). During time spent in Trentino in 1909 Mussolini met Italian socialists who lived under Austrian rule. The call for a "renewal of the Italian soul" in Mussolini's writings from that period suggests a search for political and ideological alternatives to orthodox socialism. At the same time, he was opposed to nationalism and patriotism, which he condemned together with Giolittianism. Another dominant theme from Mussolini's time in Trentino was the revolutionary polemic against parliamentary democracy (Killinger in Gentile-Di Scala 2015, pp. 143–144).

Mussolini's biographer Milza has demonstrated that it was between 1908 and 1912 that some revolutionary syndicalists began to approach the nationalist intellectuals and writers who gathered around anti-Giolittian newspapers. Mussolini, too, while not entirely converging with them, shared some of their views: the cult of action, a pragmatic philosophy, the will to change the world and forge a "new man" on the Nietzschean model. However, Mussolini was not yet converted to nationalism, as demonstrated by his writings from the time (comprising an entire volume of *Opera Omnia*, his collected works). He did recognise the patriotic roots of his political culture, the cult of Garibaldi that he received from his father, like many revolutionaries of his generation, and even wrote that the fatherland was the highest collective organism attained by ethnically civilised groups. Despite this, he differentiated between the sentiment of belonging to the nation (which he took for granted) and nationalist ideology, an invention of the bourgeoisie to legitimise its imperialistic views

(Milza 2000, pp. 130–131). What was already evident was his rejection of democracy. For example, Salvemini's and Mussolini's criticism of Giolittian democracy were animated by antithetical values, ideas, and ideals: Salvemini remained close to a humanitarian and radical socialism that he saw as being realised through legal and democratic reforms; Mussolini chose the path of violent insurrection, expressing intolerance of democracy (Killinger in Gentile-Di Scala 2015, p. 156). In an analysis of his personality, Milza has shown that Mussolini was considered an eccentric by many contemporaries, while he succeeded in creating a personality cult among groups of socialists in his region, Romagna. He often appeared excessive in both his speeches and writings; consciously launching invectives; looking for outrageous formulations, calculated vulgarity, and heavy machismo. The word *duce* was used to address him for the first time by Romagna's socialists in 1912 who regarded him as their guide (Milza 2000 p. 148).

Some historians have identified the genesis of totalitarian thought in the demonisation of the enemy during the First world War and have suggested that Mussolini was also subject to that mental process, which contributed to his anti-socialism. In fact, recent research has shown how Mussolini's progressive detachment from the PSI began before the war. In November 1913 he founded the magazine *Utopia*, where he could more freely express his ideas, including that of a possible war, than in *Avanti!*. In May 1914 *Utopia* published an article by the revolutionary syndicalist Panunzio, who argued for the necessity of a war to provoke a "revolutionary situation", supporting the idea that it was more conservative to oppose war than to support it. Analysing the correspondence between Panunzio and Mussolini and the latter's articles in the magazine, Paul O'Brien has demonstrated that Mussolini already shared this thesis, though it became more widely known following his first articles in *Il Popolo d'Italia* in autumn 1914. He interpreted the imminent Italian intervention in anti-socialist terms in his newspaper, writing, for example, that war could succeed in getting rid of a "reactionary" socialist party. As the war progressed, he became increasingly more furious with the PSI, the Bolshevik revolution, the demonstrations in Turin in 1917, and the Pope's criticism of the war. By the end of the war, the enemies of Italy were clearly identified as the socialists, who would "Caporetto" Italy again after the war (O'Brien in Isnenghi and Ceschin 2008, pp. 388–391).

As an interventionist, Mussolini maintained the patriotic-Jacobin spirit of his youth, which held an important place in the evolution of his thought during and after the war as the genesis of a national socialism that in many ways constituted the essence of the first fascism. The socialism he referred to, however, was no longer that of Marx and the socialist party. Beneath the title of *Il Popolo d'Italia*, he added two maxims: on the left-hand side of the page a sentence by the nineteenth-century French revolutionist August Blanqui ("he who has iron has bread") and on the right-hand side a citation from Napoleon ("the revolution is an idea that has found bayonets"): not by chance two

French references, since France was for left-wing interventionists the country where the ideas of revolution and war had melded (Milza p. 192; p. 205).

Historians have recently confirmed the centrality of emotion in the behaviour of the masses (Papadia 2019; Papadia and Manfredi in *Memoria e Ricerca* 2021). Radical nationalism began to appeal to the emotions of the masses more than socialism, the origins of which lay in the rationalism and positivism of the second half of the nineteenth century, and more than liberalism, which always showed a lack of interest in the masses. Le Bon and Sorel were important authors of the new political culture: they did not believe that the masses were capable of self-government, but acknowledged the importance of mass participation, and the nationalists recognised that consensus was essential in modern political action. On these terms, it was necessary for political organisations to introduce to the masses a sense of discipline and respect for hierarchy; a minority of leaders were to be venerated with a religious fervour. What socialism had done for the proletariat, the radical nationalists wanted to do for the nation and the bourgeoisie, to achieve the nationalisation of the masses (Gentile 1999, pp. 18–19). However, Mussolini's cult was created as a socialist first.

Works on the cult of Mussolini published in the 2000s mirror the shift in the 1990s from a political to a cultural history of the *duce*, in particular beginning with works by Passerini and Luzzatto. In 1991 Passerini wrote a study on the biographies of Mussolini published during his lifetime. She considered that history also includes fantasy, dreams, expectations, thoughts, and feelings, all of which can be defined as "imaginary" and intertwine, but do not coincide, with the materiality of facts. During the post-war years, anti-fascist historiography had rejected the possibility of any political or human qualities in Mussolini. But by 1990, thanks to advances in historiography, it was possible to detach and confront the subject without being accused of being nostalgic (Passerini 1991, pp. 3–5). This approach has also taken the autumn of 1914 as a key turning point, with Mussolini's transition to interventionism, his expulsion from the PSI and the publication of *Il Popolo d'Italia*. From 1915 a new image of Mussolini began to be constructed centring on his "resurrection" after the war (although he was only at the front for a few months, much propaganda was created around his war heroism and qualities of leadership), identifying him with Italy from as early as 1923, focusing on his physical person, the sacrality of his body, and the genealogy and cult of his family. This reconstruction of his image extended in the 1930s with the centralisation and control of the means of mass communication (press, cinema and radio). The media contributed to continuous praise of the *duce*, a vast quantity of biographies (often simply repetitions with no literary quality), and the additional depiction of Mussolini as war leader and founder of empire. Many of these publications were aimed at children, constructing the tale of Mussolini as a courageous child (Passerini 1991).

The idealisation surrounding Mussolini, a study by Luzzatto showed, also involved his life after death. Like Passerini, he analysed the ways in which Mussolini's body was worshipped and celebrated in contemporary publications for two decades after the march on Rome, and placed that at the centre of consensus for the regime. Luzzatto's book showed that the cult of the *duce* continued after 1945. His study, published in Italy in 1998, began with the years when Mussolini was in power, exploring the imagery surrounding the idea of the dictator's death at the point of his greatest glory. Executed by partisans at the end of the Second World War, Mussolini's body, once adored in life, was spat upon by an angry crowd and strung up in a Milan square. The corpse was subsequently buried, exhumed, stolen and hidden away for ten years, and finally buried in his native town of Predappio, which became—and continues to be—a site of pilgrimage for neo-fascists. What was the relationship between the adoring crowds in the 1920s and 1930s in the Roman square where he would appear on the balcony in front of them, and the hostile crowds that insulted his body in the square in Milan in 1945? Luzzatto investigated the meanings of the ruler's body in a totalitarian dictatorship; the charismatic nature of Mussolini's appeal; and the memory of fascism in the complex transition from dictatorship to democracy. In post-war Italy, the vicissitudes of the *duce*'s corpse fuelled sentiments of forgiveness: pitying Mussolini was a way for Italians to pity and forgive themselves (Luzzatto 1998, p. 199).

NEW STUDIES ON THE REGIME

The recent historiography has produced stimulating work not only on the origins of fascism and on Mussolini, but also on the different aspects of the dictatorship, interconnecting approaches from economic, political, social, cultural, and military history. In doing so, it has crucially engaged with the studies published by the previous generations of scholars. This section of the chapter will seek to follow such links and evolution.

A Fascist Economy?

Economic history, one of the most fertile areas of study in the 1960s and 1970s, has been marginalised since the 1980s (the years of the "cultural turn"), especially when compared with the developments that have characterised other fields. For example, the multiplication of studies on fascist architecture has shown little interest in the question of the economic resources used and of the elites that it mobilised. In the same way, a continuous debate on the nature of the consensus for the regime has ignored the issue of the financial and economic resources employed on the ground. However, contributions on different aspects of the regime's economy demonstrate how a recovery of economic history would broaden our knowledge of the regime's legitimisation and its rooting in Italian society. One victim of such neglect has been labour history, particularly the industrial and rural working class, although interest has re-emerged over the last decade, with, for example, the creation in 2012 of the Italian Society for Labour History (SISLav).

In recent decades, there has been renewed attention in Italian historiography on specific themes: for example, studies on corporativism and autarky, while mindful of the discrepancy between project and results, have paid attention to aspects of social change, overcoming the previous reductive interpretation, which described fascist corporatism as a propaganda tool only. The question of whether the regime coincided with a time of economic stagnation was raised by Valerio Castronovo at a seminar at the University of Turin as early as 1972: was there an attempt, in the interwar years, to "ruralise" Italy, privileging land ownership above industrial and financial capital? Such an interpretation, he argued, supported the idea of fascism as a parenthesis in between two periods of economic growth, while the evidence suggested that the opposite was the case: the number of employees in industry grew while the active agricultural population diminished; industrial production grew between 1921 and 1940; the collaboration between private capital and the state was strengthened (Castronovo in Quazza 1973, pp. 74–79).

A decade later, Gianni Toniolo explained how visions of a stagnant fascist economy belonged to the immediate post-war years, but had been overturned, confirming Castronovo's analysis, despite the fact that the Italian economy grew at a lower rate under fascism compared with the European average, and that wages were cut, the living standards of the lower classes fell, and consumption was reduced for most of the population (Toniolo 1980, pp. 5–7). Rolf Petri addressed these issues at the turn of the century in a book devoted to the economic history of Italy between 1918 and 1963, which analysed in detail the impact of the economic depression on Italian industry. Petri demonstrated that there was a decline in industrial output of about 20% between 1929 and 1932, with a similar decrease in industrial employment. This dramatic reduction was mitigated by agricultural underemployment and did not lead to political crisis: on the contrary, it was precisely during those years that the regime enjoyed wide support and maintained political stability, as argued by both contemporary observers and in the historiography (Petri 2002, p. 81).

Building on Petri's work, historians have subsequently analysed the relationship between politics, administration, and the technical and economic elites, with an examination of specifically fascist economic initiatives that were not necessarily failures, and that in some cases came to constitute a basis for development in the 1950s and 1960s. Until the 1990s, with few exceptions, the historiography on fascist economy had downplayed the originality of the regime's initiatives and their results. Economic programmes and ideology were initially interpreted as simply instrumental propaganda operations. As a consequence, the project for a "third way", the corporative revolution and autarkic programmes for greater independence from the world market, were analysed as failures or even pretences. However, since then, as Gagliardi has explained, scholars have explored more carefully the intentions, projects, and realisations of the regime: the idea was to take fascism seriously in the economic field as well (Gagliardi in *Studi Storici* 2014, p. 73).

Gagliardi's work on the corporative system demonstrates how it represented the instrument through which fascism sought to relate the totalitarian and authoritarian state to the plurality of interests expressed in Italian society. The corporative system was in theory an alternative to both liberal capitalism and communism through the institution of corporations (representing fascist workers, employers, and the fascist party) intended to replace the trade unions. The purpose was to try to make the national interest prevail over the interests of different classes and categories. Corporations were created, initially with the establishment of a dedicated ministry of corporations in 1926, which set out to conceive institutions for different interest groups based on fascist principles. Strikes were outlawed and the only permitted representation was that of fascist organisations. For the entrepreneurs, the corporations were a privileged channel of communication with the state (Gagliardi 2010, pp. ix–xi). The main advantage, Gagliardi has concluded, went to the industrialists, who increased their economic and political weight. By the mid-1930s the "authoritarian compromise" between the economic world and fascism strengthened, not only because of the consolidation of the regime in terms of consensus, but also due to the expansion of public intervention in the face of economic crisis. Bailouts, state commissions, and limitations on imports and competition offered help to major private companies (Gagliardi 2010, pp. 136–137).

Bruno Settis has recently reflected on the relationship between facts and propaganda by examining corporativism during the economic depression. He showed that by 1931 the crisis hit Italy harder than had long been recognised, and with a very slow recovery, as demonstrated in studies from the second decade of the 2000s, which highlighted the substantial decline in industrial production and the frustration over the rise in unemployment from 1925 onwards. In this situation, Mussolini presented the economic crisis as a crisis of liberal capitalism that fascism would challenge, demonstrating the superiority of the corporative system as a third way. Discontent among the working classes in some cases led to local protests, but these were not linked to political objectives, given the conditions of repression and the adaptation of the younger generation to the regime—something that De Felice had claimed as evidence for consensus. However, with the multiplication of public institutions, employment was granted to a middle class that was more or less able to maintain its standard of living (Settis in Albanese 2021, pp. 120–122). On the question of consumption, a recent reflection by Emanuela Scarpellini has noted an important shift since the 1980s: until then, the prevailing view was that fascism, given its military and imperialist objectives, had ignored if not actually repressed consumerism. The new research has instead revealed a more complex picture, showing that although in the 1930s publicity mostly concentrated on *italianità* (with references to ancient Rome, empire and the colonies), at the same time theatres, cinemas, low-cost rail transport, holiday camps for children and sport activities all expanded. The imagery of consumption therefore suggests elements of continuity with the post-1945 period (Scarpellini in De Luna 2022, pp. 168–171).

Settis has also reflected on whether there was a "fascist modernisation" in economic terms, defined by the relative decline of the rural economy, industrial development, the expansion of public intervention, and administrative growth. He observed how anti-fascist historiography, both contemporary with fascism and after the Second World War, had described the fascist economy as stagnant, with power left in the hands of big industrialists and a backward and parasitic class of owners. However, in his view this only partially described a more complex situation, since the regime was able to forge original institutional instruments for the organisation of credit and investment which were examples of a modern "managed economy". At the same time, it supported the preference of the industrialists to pay low wages, consolidated a low level of consumption, promoted an imbalance between urban and rural development, and abandoned the South to the margins of economic development. The poorer strata of the population became even poorer despite the welfare system (Settis in Albanese 2021, pp. 135–137).

Racism and Colonialism

After a prolonged silence, over recent decades there has been a multiplication of studies on fascism's racist and anti-Semitic policies, their links with Italian colonialism, on the construction of "otherness" with regards to colonial populations, and on the practices of racial segregation employed by the regime. Del Boca and Rochat have been for a long time among the most active historians in the debates on fascist colonialism. In the early 2000s Nicola Labanca produced two further important works on the character and practice of Italian colonialism, both from the military point of view and from the view of the conquerors and the colonisers, inserting the history of Italian imperialism into that of the regime and Italian society (Labanca 2002, 2005).

During the last two decades new studies have engaged with his work, and have continued to move beyond the simple reconstruction of events to discover in archival sources, in the contemporary press and in oral testimonies, the tangible signs of colonial society as it was planned for and implemented by the fascist government. According to Alessandro Pes, if the fascist theorisation of the construction of the "new Italian" had ever had concrete application, it must be found in the "new" societies created in the reclaimed lands (where, in the Pontine marshes, new cities were built in the 1930s, largely based on the relocation and labour of peasants from other parts of Italy) and in the colonised territories (Pes 2010, p. 7). The image of the coloniser replaced the "old" view of the Italian emigrant, as illustrated, for example, in the study conducted by Luzzatto of letters from a former emigrant turned coloniser in Ethiopia between 1936 and 1941. Through this study, Luzzato demonstrated how, for many volunteers, the motivations behind moving to the colonies were not ideological, but economic—to avoid unemployment or taxation in Italy. These expectations ended in disappointment when it became evident that Italian society simply reproduced itself in the colonies, with the corruption and bureaucracy of imperial administrations. War became the last hope for some colonisers: a fascist victory would sanction the end of a world order that condemned Italians to the role of poor emigrants (Luzzatto 2000, p. 16; p. 25).

The reality of war and its outcome obviously undermined that prospect, but, as Emanuele Ertola has suggested, it would be a mistake to attribute the causes of such disappointment only to its tragic end. Those who moved to Africa after 1936 soon realised that the empire was not a land of opportunity, and that the fascist authorities were incapable of governing it effectively (Ertola 2017, pp. 235–236). Research into the realities of fascist control of the colonies has also demonstrated that the regime had endemic management problems due to its lack of real control, since Ethiopian insurrectionary resistance was never quelled after 1936. Consequently, contemporary knowledge of the real social situation in the colonies was scarce thanks to the dynamics of power in the fascist government. The colonial ruling class tended to sweeten its reports to Rome, fearing that a truthful analysis would be regarded negatively at the centre and could have local repercussions for them (Pes 2010, p. 13).

In a recent historiographical overview, Valeria Deplano has argued that colonial policies had long been treated as a marginal chapter in the history of fascism. Colonialism should instead be considered a structural element in the regime's history. From the 1920s until the Second World War the government invested both economic and propaganda resources in a colonial policy with Africa at its centre. The state-nation building process was thus intertwined with the construction of empire (Deplano in Albanese 2021, pp. 46–47). Operations described by Labanca as genocidal, like that led by general (from 1935 marshal) Graziani in Cyrenaica against a precisely defined ethnic group (the nomadic and semi-nomadic populations of Gebel and of the desert), showed how extreme violence had become a characteristic element in the colonies (Labanca 2012). Ignoring the tragic impact such tactics had on the civilian populations, the regime focused on spreading colonial propaganda through schools and youth movements, exhibitions on the colonies and the exploitation of cinema seeking to reach the whole nation. From this perspective, the war in Ethiopia was not a moment of rupture in fascist history, but one of continuity, the perfecting of a long-term project. At the same time, it represented a turning point, signalling a break with the democracies and bringing Italy into line with Nazi Germany.

Through mobilisation at home, which involved large parts of the population (for example, with the collection of wedding rings to help fund the colonial effort), historians agree that Africa became part of national life and 1936 the point at which the regime achieved its widest consensus. The reality in Ethiopia was not what Italians were told, however: the Ethiopian resistance was staunch and complicated the military-police operations after 1936, leading to deportations, imprisonment, and summary executions under Graziani. Research has brought violence to the heart of reflections on Italian and fascist colonialism (Deplano in Albanese 2021, p. 56–61).

Historians have also connected the history of Italian colonialism with that of fascist racism. Important steps have been taken since the 1960s. The impact of the alliance with Nazi Germany has been minimised, remaining in the background of research that has mainly concentrated over the past twenty years on the Italian context. David Bidussa has shown that anti-Semitism in Italy did not suddenly appear in 1938 in the shape of a set of laws, but was based on components that were already present in Italian culture and society: it was, in other words, an Italian discourse, not an Italian translation from the German (Bidussa 1994, p. 19).

One fundamental aspect of this argument has been to see the connection between imperial and anti-Semitic policies: the conquest of Ethiopia marked the transition from a racist colonialism to a purely racist policy, with the promulgation of racist laws in 1937 discriminating against Africans and forbidding any mixing between the races. One of the most influential historians in this field was Enzo Collotti, whose work led to reconsideration not only of the history of racism and anti-Semitism, but also of the choices made by the fascist regime in foreign policy. Collotti read the fascist policy against the Jews as an integral part of the history of fascism—especially as one of the characteristic aspects of the totalitarian shift of the 1930s—but also of Italian society under the regime, analysing anew Italian attitudes towards the racist laws and their application (Collotti 2006, p. 3; pp. 80–101).

Building on this historiography, the work of Michele Sarfatti, from an important 1994 volume to more recent publications, has investigated aspects of the anti-Semitic legislation and the impact it had on Jews living in Italy. He has demonstrated that fascist measures were not improvised, but were inserted into a protracted programme of racism from the Ethiopian war onwards (Duranti 2019, p. 12; p. 14). Sarfatti emphasised the ways in which racist laws were put into practice, and how 1938 heralded the transition from a complex policy of Jewish discrimination to a violent policy of persecution, with a further transition under the Mussolini's Social Republic of 1943–45, from the persecution of rights to the persecution of lives (Sarfatti 1994, p. 6).

An important addition came from Valeria Galimi, who has explored the reactions of the Italian people to the racist laws, observing that Italians were not immune from racism and anti-Semitism. She has challenged the idea that the consensus around fascism declined because of the racist laws; Italians (and the catholic Church) supported the racist turn that accompanied the conquest of Ethiopia in 1936 (Galimi 2018, pp. 15–16). In her view, it is impossible to agree either with an image of a totally racist Italian society or of an entire society that expressed solidarity and generosity towards Jews; in general, Italians lived with anti-Semitism easily enough. For example, in certain economic sectors, companies worried about the economic impact of the laws, but this did not result in attempts to counter them. In the same way, universities simply applied the legislation and replaced expelled Jewish teachers. Of course, threats from the regime against anyone who sided with the Jews also played a role in dissuading the population from expressing discontent (Galimi 2018, pp. 19–26).

Consideration of the centrality of colonialism and racism to the fascist project also came from historians interested in the fascist use of the past. For example, in a book edited by Paola Salvatori in 2020, Laurence Haack described how the history of the Etruscans served the imperatives of the colonial war from the mid-1930s, because they were defined in works by fascist historians as a people with mixed blood, who should no longer be studied. In the same volume, Alessandro Cavagna delineated the ways in which the conquest of Ethiopia and the submission of its population were described at the "Exhibition of *romanità*" [Roman-ness] in 1937 in ways designed to create parallels between the age of Augustus and Mussolini's Rome, capital of an empire once more (Haack and Cavagna in Salvatori 2020, p. 33; p 58). Historical remains were also employed in the "machine of the consensus", when Roman ruins in Africa were exploited as signs of *italianità* abroad. In the second half of the 1930s in particular, references to ancient Rome became an obsession in attempts to incorporate its overseas history and geography into the current narrative of the imperial nation. Antiquities and ancient monuments in the colonies became the "exclusive benefit" of the Italian colonisers, contributing to the birth of a national-colonial heritage inherently connected to Italian ambitions for power (Troilo 2021, pp. 12–13; p. 212).

The Regime's Foreign Policy

Collotti was one of the first historians to insist on the need to connect the trajectory of fascist foreign policy towards territorial expansion with the regime's ideological premises. His point of departure was the conviction that fascist foreign policy could not be explained in isolation from the nature of the regime that promoted it (Collotti 2000). Salvemini had already drawn a connection between the regime's foreign policy actions and the search for consensus at home. Although subsequent historiography has highlighted the strictly ideological standpoint of Salvemini's analysis (which was written before archival documentation was available), it has also confirmed some important aspects, among them fascist opposition to democratic France, Mussolini's desire to revise the geopolitical system created at Versailles, and his opposition to the League of Nations. Fascist revisionism applied especially to the future of the Balkans and North Africa, an interpretation already confirmed by Ennio Di Nolfo, who published one of the first works on Mussolini's foreign policy in 1960.

In this field, too, there has emerged in the past decades a historiography that challenges De Felice's analysis of Italian foreign policy. De Felice's interpretation was largely based on the papers of Dino Grandi, former foreign minister (1929–1932) and ambassador to London (1932–1939), which were used to support the theory of the "determining weight", according to which Mussolini appeared as mediator between the democracies and Hitler, uncertain about which side to take until as late as 1939. This thesis was already contradicted at the time by Collotti, who emphasised the fascist character of the regime's diplomacy and foreign policy as well as its anti-democratic and revisionist campaign against the League of Nations from Mussolini's invasion of Corfu in 1923 until Italy's exit from the League in 1937. The critique continued in the 1980s with the American historian MacGregor Knox, who demonstrated Grandi's post-fascist attempt to present himself (with De Felice's support) as a virtually non-fascist diplomat, a position helped by the fact that Grandi's autobiographical writings were published without any critical revision (Knox in *Passato e Presente* 1987, pp. 98–117). With the opening of Grandi's unpublished papers in the archives from the late 1990s, it was finally possible to verify his actions against Britain during the Ethiopian war and to reveal Mussolini's anti-British foreign policy from 1935 (Baldoli 2003).

Elena Aga Rossi placed Italian diplomatic activity in an international context, linking it to fascist imperialism in Africa (Aga Rossi in Sabbatucci-Vidotto 1995–1999). A book by Collotti, published in 2000, with a contribution by Labanca, focused on the fascist characteristics of the regime's diplomacy and foreign policy, partly building on a 1995 work by Nicola Tranfaglia, who explored the links between domestic and foreign policy (Tranfaglia 1995). Knox has been another supporter of the idea of a coherent thread in fascist foreign policy. His 1995 book *Common Destiny*, linking the fascist and Nazi international projects (translated into Italian in 2003), stressed the centrality of Italian military expansionism in fascism and the elements of continuity with previous Italian foreign policy (in particular, aspirations in the Balkans and North Africa). Like Collotti, Knox criticised De Felice's assumptions about Rome's equidistance between London and Berlin on the lines of Grandi's thesis of the "determining weight" and the view that Mussolini was forced to wage war on Ethiopia and ally himself with Hitler only because of British intransigence. Finally, Davide Rodogno has focused on the central place of fascist Italy's plans for expanded power in the Mediterranean basin, which has undermined De Felice's reading of a fascism that hesitated between Britain and Germany—as if lacking its own project—until the outbreak of war (Rodogno 2006).

Recent studies have investigated another aspect of Italian diplomacy, strictly linked to its foreign policy: the attempt by fascism to "export" its model and ideology abroad, both to Italian emigrant communities and to foreign fascist movements. In a thorough overview, Matteo Pretelli reconstructed the links between Italians abroad and fascism, examining the regime's migration policies and the response of the emigrants. He showed how the project for the fascistisation of Italian expat communities evolved with the war in Ethiopia and the regime's expansionist claims. This involved not only collaboration with foreign fascist movements, but also the promotion of Italian propaganda, schools and summer camps for children abroad (Pretelli 2010). The relationship between fascism abroad and imperialism was considered in studies, such as that by Deborah Paci, which focused on the regime's interest in expanding into other territories such as Malta and Corsica, but also Tunisia and Egypt (Paci 2015). These studies have emphasised how fascist cultural diplomacy abroad connected with the regime's expansionist projects (Cavarocchi 2010, p. 9). Links between foreign policy, propaganda and emigration are therefore contributory factors in explaining the development of Mussolini's revisionist foreign policy.

The Fascist Wars

In 2005, Rochat exposed what he regarded as an insufficient dialogue between historiography on fascism and on the war: how was it possible to consider a historical event separately from its outcome? The vicissitudes of the fascist wars should be considered fundamental to understanding the two decades preceding them, and they revealed the character of the regime in many ways. In his study of the fascist press and of Mussolini's speeches, Isnenghi has argued that the regime felt and presented itself as continuously at war. This sense of a system under siege was propagated both within and outside Italy for the entire duration of the regime (Isnenghi 1989, pp. 36–50).

The tendency in post-war Italian public discourse was to suppress the memory of 1940–1943—an iniquitous and unnatural war driven by Mussolini's alliance with Hitler—and instead to memorialise the years 1943–1945, an Italian war on the side of the Allies in which Italians could be presented as the victims of Nazi Germany. One of the first attempts to reconsider the fascist war of 1940–1943 was undertaken through a series of conferences in the 1980s and the 1990s, particularly that organised in Brescia by the Foundation Luigi Micheletti in 1989, which contributed to inserting the years 1940–1943 into the more general history of fascism and of Italy. During that conference, Knox claimed that a global interpretation of the origins of the fascist war was still lacking. Such an interpretation, he argued, should focus on three aspects: to explore Mussolini's foreign policy and ideology from the 1920s, without excluding (as De Felice had) the existence of a programme of conquest; to link the regime's domestic and foreign policies; and to analyse the history of Italian foreign policy, not only in diplomatic terms, but also from the viewpoint of the economy and military strategy, leaving aside explanations that rested on the dictator's opportunism or on his personality and emotional state (Knox in *Annali* 1990–1991, p. 17).

Rochat also pointed to an absence of detailed studies of the Italian military effort. His own research in the national military archives demonstrated aspects that further studies, both by himself and other historians, would confirm in later years: that the regime, despite two decades of propaganda about Italy's imperial power, had been incapable from the beginning of mobilising forces effectively, and that the operational capacity of the armed forces diminished as the war progressed (Rochat in *Annali* 1990–1991, p. 35). Specific research was also presented on the Italian occupation of Greece and Yugoslavia, planting the seeds for a wealth of studies that have appeared in recent years (among them, Osti Guerrazzi 2011; Fonzi 2019).

Another field opened during the conference was the relationship between war and public opinion, which was examined by Simona Colarizi using fascist political police records in the national archives in Rome. She confirmed the position expressed up to then by most of the historiography, that 1938 was the beginning of the crisis in the consensus: with the fear of another war looming and a general dissatisfaction about the alliance with Hitler's Germany, trust in the regime was subject to a general decline. The first few weeks of enthusiasm expressed in Italian cities after the declaration of war against Britain and France in June 1940 reflected the hope that the war could be won quickly. Popular sentiment soon turned to indifference at the outcome of the conflict and a detachment from the regime on the part of a majority of the population. As support for the regime declined, Allied propaganda strengthened, and listening to the BBC services for Italy (principally *Radio Londra*) became a mass phenomenon, illustrating that Italians no longer trusted information propagated by the regime (Colarizi in *Annali* 1990–1991, pp. 657–666).

Since that seminal conference, historians have interrogated the wartime relationship between fascism and business groups, the failure of industrial mobilisation, the military crisis, and the collapse of the internal front. As Lucio Ceva argued ten years later, industrialists did not seriously engage in the fascist war and, as a result, the regime was unable to mobilise major industries to the necessary extent (Ceva 1999, pp. 276–277). Mussolini's fear of losing popularity meant that no changes in mobilisation levels could be imposed domestically even after he had decided to enter the war in 1940 at the time of Germany's victorious campaign in France. Despite requests from the armed forces, the dictator avoided attempts at imposing military discipline on the industrial working class until January 1943, in stark contrast with the liberal ruling elite's actions during the First World War (Knox 2002, pp. 43–44).

Italy's problem was not simply a question of resources, but also one of military culture. There was a gaping chasm between the regime's military ambitions, its propaganda campaigns, its image as an internationally competitive armed force, and its actual industrial and economic strength (Rochat 2008, p. 231). Although commander-in-chief Badoglio, together with the three chiefs of staff of the navy, army and air force, had warned Mussolini about the country's insufficient preparation, the decision to declare war was based on purely political considerations, as if politics was an independent variable *vis-a-vis* military capability: Mussolini seemed convinced that Britain and France would lose the war and that it would therefore be in Italy's interest to take part, so that it could enter a never-ending cycle of victories and profit from a subsequent peace settlement.

Historians have finally confirmed Rochat's early interpretation, showing that the conditions under which Italy entered the war in 1940 were not comparable to those of May 1915, when Italy had joined an international coalition supported by colossal empires. Instead, between 1940 and 1943, its German ally, crushed by its own growing demands for resources, could not provide Italy with enough material and military assistance to guarantee its survival.

Moreover, while at the time of the battle of Vittorio Veneto in 1918 the armed forces had fought with substantially improved weapons and equipment compared with what had been available in 1915, at the time of the armistice in 1943 soldiers had to fight under conditions that had barely changed from those of June 1940 with weapons many of which dated from the First World War (Baldoli in Albanese 2021, pp. 69–92).

The assessment of reasons for the military defeat, however, has not meant an underestimation of the impact of the Italian wars in terms of violence on the civilian populations of the invaded countries, nor of the fascist project for a new Mediterranean order. One example is that of the Spanish Civil War. Begun as military, strategic, and diplomatic assistance to Francisco Franco, the fascist intervention soon made Italy a belligerent country in the conflict. As Javier Rodrigo has demonstrated, once the initial coup d'état plan had failed, the *Corpo Truppe Volontarie* (fascist voluntary troops) was created to help Franco, and also as a tool to build fascist Spain and, indeed, a fascist Europe. The Spanish Civil War was first internationalised because of Mussolini, and can be called a European civil war also because of the intervention of the fascist dictatorships, which gave it a clear ideological character. However, Spanish historiography has neglected the Italian intervention since the prevailing view was of an Italian army composed of ragamuffins, cowards and good-hearted people, constructing what Rodrigo has called the "Guadalajara syndrome"—from the Italian defeat in the battle of Guadalajara in March 1937 (Rodrigo in *War in History*, 2019, pp. 86–104). This study fits in well with many works on the Italian wars that take seriously the fascist geo-political revisionist project.

Historians have also drawn a link between military and colonial history, considering Ethiopia as a laboratory for the project of Italian expansion in the Second World War. Some recent works have broadened this to consider the occupation of Yugoslavia and Greece, investigating the repression of the civilian populations and the forms of resistance to Italian occupation. Italian war crimes during the colonial wars and the Second World War have constituted the most complex aspect in the relationship between historians and public opinion, as shown by those who have examined the refusal of many Italians—supported by right-wing political parties—to face up to their country's past. These works have also confronted the question of memory and oblivion in the public use of history, drawing, particularly from the 1990s, on work by Nicola Gallerano (Gallerano 1995).

Filippo Focardi has argued that the cliché of the "evil German", common to the whole of Europe, was not the only element in establishing the public memory and image of Italians after the end of the war: it was also associated from the start with the popular self-image of the "good-hearted Italian". The image of the German soldier, viewed as a disciplined sadist and bloodthirsty combatant, was counterposed to that of the Italian soldier, adverse to war and acts of aggression, ready to bring solidarity and support even to the populations of countries his regime had occupied. A hegemonic account was thus generated, and propagated through popular culture, which minimised or even denied the

Italian people's involvement with fascism and the country's responsibility for the fascist war and its crimes, especially in the Balkans. The absence of an "Italian Nuremberg" against Italian war criminals sanctioned that depiction. The stereotype, like all stereotypes, was based on some historically-founded facts: it was true that the atrocities committed by the Germans were quantitatively larger and qualitatively more severe than those that weighed on the Italian conscience; and it was true that Italian soldiers in occupied countries did rescue thousands of Jews and Serbs threatened with death by the Germans and their Ustasha Croat allies. However, the stereotype concealed the other side of the coin, in particular the numerous war crimes perpetrated by the Italian army against both partisans and civilians in occupied territories, or Italian involvement in the German persecution of the Jews even before the Social Republic (Focardi 2013, pp. x–xi; xiii). It has been possible through United Nations sources to suggest a figure of around 250,000 victims of the Italian occupation in Yugoslavia and 100,000 in Greece. Through a study of the correspondence of Italian soldiers and of Italian secret police reports, historians have also demonstrated Italian participation in acts of cruelty and their appreciation for ruthless German methods against resistance activity and populations that were deemed to be uncivilised (Focardi 2013, pp. 132–133).

The process of "externalisation" of the violent and criminal side of the regime, noted Focardi, contributed to the "retroactive defascistisation" of the fascist dictatorship discussed by Gentile in 2002. Historians have now thoroughly dismantled the myths of the good-hearted Italian and of fascism as a benevolent regime, by unearthing not only the aspects of violence and repression at home, but also the massacres in the colonies, the racist policies against Slavs, Africans and Jews, the military occupations during the Axis war with the harsh treatment against civilians that accompanied them, the mass deportations of men, women and children, and the absence of punishment for Italian war criminals. However, the results of historical research have had only superficial effects on public opinion (Focardi 2013, p. 183; p. 187).

The historiography of the last 15 years has also focused on the Italians' reaction to Allied bombing in the Second World War. This has revealed the failure of the regime both in military terms and in terms of the relationship between regime and civilian population, and has led to further critical reflections on the question of consensus. The Allied bombing of Italy between 1940 and 1945 caused around 60,000 civilian deaths, two-thirds of which took place when Italy was no longer an enemy after the armistice of September 1943. It was unquestionably the most devastating experience for the population in large parts of the peninsula. It is useful to ask what Italians must have thought under heavy bombardment, left defenceless by their own government and by the local authorities, and subject to propaganda from the Allies-invaders who presented themselves as powerful and invincible liberators. The Allies sent messages of friendship through leaflets dropped from aircraft or via BBC radio, inciting Italians to rebel against a militarily inept vaudeville dictatorship that had deceived them and forced them into alliance with their age-old enemy, a regime that had revealed its military ineptitude despite preparing Italians for war for almost two decades.

At the time when Italians were being bombed, the country had been an aggressor for years, in addition to fighting alongside Nazi Germany until 1943. Early defeats and the realisation that the country was not prepared for conflict could not fail to subject the regime and its German alliance to criticism; with the loss of Cyrenaica in January 1941, Italians living in what was called the "critical" area of the country, i.e., the industrial cities of the north, also started to consider Mussolini's personal responsibility. British messages appealing to the memories of the First World War to remind Italians of their "age-old" enemy found a receptive audience from the start, but especially from autumn 1942, when the population began to detach itself from the fascist war and to pay attention to Anglo-American appeals, which sought to persuade Italians that supporting fascism had been a mistake, even instilling a sense of guilt (Baldoli in Albanese 2021, pp. 85–90). As Gabriella Gribaudi suggested, it was not so much the bombs that caused a collapse in morale, but first and foremost the revelation that the fascist state was impotent Gribaudi in Baldoli, Knapp and Overy 2011, pp. 219–237). In many ways, the war and its conduct on both the military and home fronts can be considered a logical outcome of the regime where military rhetoric failed to match a limited military reality.

Reconsidering the Consensus

Among the concepts introduced by De Felice in the 1970s the most significant was that of mass consensus in favour of the regime, which provoked intensive debate among historians and the public alike. Few historians would now deny the existence of a consensus: debates surround its periodisation, quality and intensity, and duration. Recent works on internal confinement, the role of the judiciary, and violence under the regime, for example by Camilla Poesio, Leonardo Pompeo D'Alessandro and Michael Ebner, explained how squad violence assumed the role of a kind of informal government (Poesio 2011; D'Alessandro 2020; Ebner 2011). In his biography of Mussolini, Milza showed how, in order to obtain support among at least part of the population, the dictatorship could count on a police control apparatus that other regimes would later imitate and perfect, but which was utilised effectively for the first time in Italy (Milza 2000, p. 618). All this clearly limits the extent to which it is possible to talk about consensus.

At the same time, mapping the existence and breadth of dissent under fascism has not proved an easy task: not only did organised opposition (and thus repressed or clandestine) spread in Italian society, but a spontaneous dissention also widened. Colarizi noticed the need to study this in the 1970s, moving beyond the hagiographic view of the heroic minority who opposed fascism from a position of illegality, from exile, or during the Resistance (Colarizi 1976, p. 2). Intertwining fascist police sources with oral history in a study of the Turin working class during fascism, Passerini demonstrated the cultural—rather than directly political—opposition to fascism among factory workers, shedding light on the relationship between the masses and power structures. She concluded that it was not possible to deduce consensus from a lack of political opposition or, in turn, to define forms of cultural opposition as dissent. The relationship of ordinary people with a totalitarian power was characterised by complex and deep contradictions, also on a psychological level, especially for a working class that shared different cultures, influenced in part by intellectuals and scientists of the industrial age, but also by ancient popular traditions (Passerini 1984, pp. 5–6).

Moreover, the regime was not simply the result of a violent fascist elite that imposed itself on a majority of anti-fascists. The problem of understanding the relationship between regime and people was forcefully presented by Gallerano in a 1986 article criticising anti-fascism as a canon of historiographical interpretation. He suggested the need for a profound revision of the scholarship, in particular with regards to the relationship between anti-fascism and Italian society during the interwar years (Gallerano 1986). As D'Alessandro has emphasised, the assumption of anti-fascism as a fundamental value of the Republic in the post-war years contributed to the elimination of the question of whether there had been consensus for fascism. This in turn implied the construction of a form of "innocence" on the part of the entire Italian people for Mussolini's dictatorship, and contributed to creating a public memory that lacked any reflection on its fascist past (D'Alessandro in *Studi Storici*, 2014, pp. 197–211). The identity value of the Resistance came to the fore in lively polemics during the first half of the 1990s, with the dissolution of the parties that had constituted the "first Republic" (1946–1994). As Luzzatto has argued, anti-fascism was undergoing a profound crisis, partly because the general conviction shared by the media and the leaders of the new political parties was that fascism no longer existed. This led to the idea that Italy could develop a shared memory, forgetting the divisions of the past, a seemingly impossible task, considering that the division between fascists and anti-fascists was not bridgeable. How could the history and values of perpetrators be reconciled with those of their victims? (Luzzatto 2004, pp. 25–26).

Military historians have also contributed to the debate, investigating consensus for fascism among the armed forces. A recent work by Fabio De Ninno on the navy during fascism criticised the view (supported by De Felice, but also by other historians) that the military remained first and foremost loyal to the monarchy and was only partially influenced by fascism. He revealed instead the tight links between the navy and fascist foreign policy (De Ninno 2017, pp. ix–xi). Similarly, there has been an examination on the attitude of Italian industrialists. While the support they gave to fascism from the beginning is not in question, the extent of their consensus has been debated. In particular, although they did not voice any opposition, industrialists appeared to react with preoccupation to the outbreak of the Second World War and Italian participation; as Luciano Segreto explained, they began to be worried as early as the 1930s, following the alliance with Germany (Segreto 1997, pp. 163–167). From

1940, some of them began to think about the need for a new institutional system, as well as for the exit from the war. This, coupled with Mussolini's fears of losing consensus among the population, explains why in 1940 there was no national mobilisation: universities did not close, nor did the stock exchange, not even the football championship (except for 1943–1944).

Between the end of the 1980s and the beginning of the 1990s, historians also began to rediscover Gramsci's reflections on the breadth and depth of the masses' involvement with fascism (D'Alessandro in *Studi Storici*, 2014, p. 200). This was a complex question, Milza argued, in light of the fact that the lower and middle classes who suffered because of unemployment, wage constriction, rises in the cost of living and escalating taxation, nevertheless continued to support the regime and its leader. The omnipresent propaganda, which made use of all the modern means of communication, together with the pervasiveness of the party's organisational institutions and police control were not sufficient explanations for a consensus that existed until at least 1937. A strong element in reinforcing that consensus was the cult of Mussolini and the religion of the *patria*, expressed among other means through the mass rallies addressed by the *duce*, as well as a general pride regarding Italy's prestige abroad—as it was represented by the regime, at least. The peasants certainly did not gain from fascist policies: in continuity with the liberal state, Mussolini's regime invested mainly in industrialisation and favoured the agrarian elite in terms of tax advantages and state subsidies. At the same time, Mussolini portrayed the peasant world as the model for Italians, the repository of the virtues of the Italian race, the world that had given Italy its First World War soldiers. The welfare state, certainly more developed than in the liberal period, and organisations such as the afterwork clubs, contributed to people's participation in the life of the regime. The lower classes lived a difficult life, but they had also done so before fascism, so it was possible for the regime, using all the means at its disposal, to maintain support even during the economic crisis (Milza 2000, pp. 652–655).

One aspect of the consensus on which Isnenghi had already focused in the 1970s was the cult of Mussolini. For Emilio Gentile, too, the myth of Mussolini was a fundamental component of fascism and one of the most popular of the regime's mythologies. The crisis of liberal democracy between the wars led many to prefer charismatic leaders to dull bourgeois politicians. This was also true for socialism, where the first cult of Mussolini emerged, only to be transformed in nationalist terms during the war and then exalted by the consensus factory after the conquest of power and throughout the regime. A recent example of the consensus debate was presented by the American *Journal of Modern Italian Studies*, which in 2014 published a review by Gentile on two new books by Christopher Duggan (2012) and Paul Corner (2012), their responses and some final comments by Gentile. The research conducted by Corner (based largely on fascist police files) concentrated on the theme of consensus through a study of the party, concluding that the fall in support for fascism before the war, around 1938, was due to the incapacity of the party to keep it alive. According to Corner, the apparent consensus among the population was a fundamental instrument for the regime. Duggan shifted attention to the perspective from below; most of his sources were diaries and the correspondence of ordinary Italians. Public opinion had already been the focus of other historians, for example Colarizi, who uncovered—as Passerini had done in her work on Turin—the existence of anti-fascist sentiment in the 1930s which could not easily be expressed in political terms (Colarizi 1991). Duggan explored the ramifications of the cult of the *duce*, which were complex and served as an element of cohesion. The wish to keep Mussolini's image uncontaminated was powerful and managed to coexist with the tendency to blame the failures of fascism (especially the military disaster of 1940–1943) not on the *duce*, but on the party or on other fascist leaders around him.

Following work by scholars such as Mabel Berezin (1997) or Ruth Ben Ghiat (2001), who focused on mass culture and the emotional aspects of the consensus, Gagliardi has recently paid attention to the role of the means of mass communication in influencing how individuals lived their relationship with politics and elaborated the regime's propaganda. While cultural media consumption did not entirely replace pre-existing cultures and mentalities, it nevertheless helps to explain decisive aspects of the dynamics of consensus expressed towards the dictatorship (Gagliardi in Albanese 2021, p. 255–279). A useful contribution also came from Salvatore Lupo, who discussed what he named "the many faces of the consensus". He has suggested that even the use of the term consensus is debateable when applied to a repressive regime that left no space for anti-fascism, while it magnified its own achievements without the possibility of any counterinformation, so that a large section of public opinion became convinced by the propaganda. Lupo has argued that historians should distinguish between the vast range of possible attitudes, which, in different situations, geographical areas and periods included indifference, forms of opposition, conformist acceptance or militant participation. Rethinking De Felice's idea of consensus to fascism, Lupo agreed that its peak was during the years that followed the Great Depression, and that the regime emerged strengthened from the crisis. De Felice had argued that the regime achieved in the 1930s a much deeper consensus than the liberal state had ever done, a comparison between liberalism and dictatorship that Lupo regarded as rather strained. Instead of consensus it was, in his opinion, more a question of nation-building through the insertion of the lower classes into public life, something that would be inevitably more advanced in 1936 (both in Italy and elsewhere) than at the time of Unification or just before the First World War. For example, in the 1930s new legislation included paid holidays, sick leave and family benefits but this did not significantly reduce the reserved attitude of industrial workers towards the regime. There was also a generational gap, as young workers were more willing than older ones to accept the regime: in the memories of those who were young at the time, a large part is played by sports activities, dances hosted in party premises, or the previously unknown experience of seaside holidays at summer camps organised by the party. The dimension of free time, which the party successfully exploited, played a large part in the construction of consensus, which went together with an appreciation for public works and architecture, admiration for Italian transatlantic flights, the uniformed gatherings in city squares, and the sound of Mussolini's voice blaring from the radio or public loudspeakers. Between the two minorities of fascist and anti-fascist militants, a majority of young people in the 1930s considered fascism the expression of a new Italy and a model of modernity, despite the regime's strong emphasis on discipline (Lupo 2000, pp. 329–332).

The difficulty in defining consensus under a totalitarian system is very well exemplified in a book by Giovanni De Luna on anti-fascism in Italian society from 1922 to 1939. He has examined not only organised anti-fascism, which was the preserve of only a small minority, but also the limits to totalitarianism posed by hegemonic forces that pre-existed the regime, such as the monarchy, the army, economic interests, and the Vatican. He has added to these what he calls "existential anti-fascism". The regime's aim to absorb the whole social body of the country by unifying society with the institutions of public life was obstructed from below through the persistence of familial and communal networks that remained more important to ordinary people than the party's organisations. The working class continued to prefer the spontaneous socialisation of the neighbourhood and the local pub (*osteria*) to the forced socialisation of the party's afterwork organisation. Building on work by Mariuccia Salvati, he also found that even public employees interpreted their position within the party as corporate workers rather than as militants pursuing a specific national mission (De Luna 1995, pp. 35–38; Salvati 1992).

In conclusion, as Isnenghi remarked, the consensus existed, but it remains difficult to measure it precisely, not least because it is possible to express consensus only when there is also freedom to express dissent (Isnenghi 2011a, b, p. 197).

Centre and Periphery, State and Party

A wealth of new works on the relationship between the state and the party, on the welfare state, and on the role of women have all contributed in many ways to answering the questions concerning the degree of consensus and the extent of totalitarian control. A volume edited by Corner and Galimi in 2014 demonstrated that the problem of many local histories of fascism was the tendency towards isolation, because they failed to explain aspects of the regime at a national level. One suggestion was to analyse the relationship between the party at both local and national levels with the ministries and the state bureaucracy. According to its totalitarian project, fascism sought to control the provinces, presenting itself as a unitary body in which independent local initiatives would be impossible. However, at the local level, profound tensions emerged that had an impact at the centre, provoking continuous negotiation and mediation between the two. Recent studies have focused, for example, on institutions such as ONMI (the National Organisation for Maternity and Childhood), GUF (University Fascist Groups) or the fascist trade unions, which did not act locally simply as mere executors of orders received from Rome, but constructed complex and dynamic relationships with the centre (Corner and Galimi 2014).

Further studies produced in the first two decades of the twenty-first century have contributed to overcoming an idea, rooted in the 1970s, of a fascist party subjugated to the state and losing political weight in the localities. These studies made use of research on fascism at local level conducted from the early 1990s by historians close to the historical institutes of the Resistance, who also analysed the relationship between centre and periphery and concluded that the party's role was not hollowed out under the regime, but was sometimes even reinforced as, for example, in the case of the regime's welfare organisation. Between the 1980s and the early 1990s, historical institutes of the Resistance across Italy promoted new studies on fascism's provincial and regional dimensions. An article by Gallerano in 1991 showed how the PNF became an important instrument of intervention locally thanks to its social assistance activities, capable of influencing the balance of power between centre and periphery (Gallerano 1991, p. 392). As later demonstrated by Baris, the subordination of the *federali* (party chiefs) to the prefects (who represented the state locally) did not eliminate local power clashes (Baris in *Studi Storici* 2014, p. 31).

Marco Palla has since expressed the difficulty of separating party and state because they were not antagonists but the components of a "state-party" in which the party contributed its own political energy to the decision-making process (Palla 2001, pp. 7–8). Lupo endorsed this conclusion by examining the role of party leaders and prefects when together carrying out epurations in the party at the local level, highlighting the fact that prefects had often enjoyed a parallel career in the party, and disproving the idea of any "easy contradictions" between fascism and the state (Lupo 2000, p. 263).

A Fascist Welfare State?

The same issues can be analysed through investigations into the fascist welfare state. Until the 1980s, there was a general prejudice against the idea of the fascist welfare state as anything more than an instrument for social control. From the 1990s, historians have attempted to measure the gap between the regime's propaganda and what was actually implemented in terms of social assistance, insurance, and health. In a 1994 article, Salvati made reference to the "centrality of the fascist experience" in the long-term history of the Italian social state (Salvati in *Passato e presente* 1994, p. 24). Together with research conducted by Michela Minesso in 2015, she also helped to highlight the aspects of continuity between fascism and the post-war period, when a system of patronage established by the fascist state was developed and intensified. In the 1930s the regime expanded social provision organisationally and increased the number of people registered for welfare. There was a strong party presence in all the institutions devoted to social assistance, and one of the priorities was to consolidate fascist control over society.

The new research has shown the discretionary character of fascist welfare, which was not universally extended to all citizens as in European democracies, but provided as concessions to particular social sectors, especially among the middle classes: for example, peasants were excluded from unemployment insurance. Local authorities possessed significant discretionary powers over who would qualify for assistance, which often ended up as little more than "charity". ONMI and services for families were particularly important in the consolidation of the regime and its demographic policies (Giorgi in *Studi Storici* 1914, pp. 93–107).

In her investigation into the welfare state in fascist Italy, Minesso found certain continuities between liberal Italy, the interwar years, and the post-war Republic. Legislation on themes of work, social insurance, national health, literacy, and popular housing was particularly developed during the Giolittian age, even though the state never devoted sufficient economic resources for the programmes. The fascist regime continued along the same path and sought to adapt the legislation to a general European trend for international welfare organisations, for example, in the area of child protection. She has concluded that the fascist development of a social state was part of a general European process, though interpreted according to its totalitarian character. The regime's social provisions were indeed linked to its aims of national greatness and racial superiority (Minesso 2015, pp. 10–13).

Women in the Fascist Regime

Gender history too has provided a useful contribution to the discussion on consensus. Italian gender historians have found the contributions from the Anglo-Saxon world particularly beneficial, especially the work by Victoria De Grazia (1992) and Perry Willson (2002). De Grazia explored the contradictions in women's experience during fascism, which provided new opportunities for public activities in its female organisations, such as the *fasci femminili*, while at the same time subjecting women to new forms of repression; fascism provided glimpses of modernity while limiting it through tradition. Fascism wanted women to be confined to their role as mothers and to restore the patriarchal authority that had been challenged by the growth of feminism during the liberal period and by the central role that women had assumed during the First World War. Above all, it wanted to solve the demographic crisis of falling birth-rates common to all of Europe, a campaign that Mussolini undertook from the late 1920s. The negation of women's emancipation went together with reforms for the social protection of mothers and children, with the institution of mass organisations for women, and with legal restrictions on contraception and abortion.

There remained a gap, however, between the regime's ambitions on gender issues and the social reality. Indeed, the attitude of women during fascism, insofar as it is possible to reconstruct it, shows that they were not simply passive and hopeless victims: the response to fascist domination appears more complex than simply an oscillation between passive subordination and ecstatic enthusiasm. Apprehension, rebellion, dissimulation, scepticism, and a growing awareness of their rights as women and citizens were widespread (De Grazia 1993, p. 28; p. 31). The principal effect of the repression of contraception, and the absence of information about birth control was a step towards recourse to clandestine abortion, which took place in conditions of inadequate hygiene and led to infections, permanent damage, and death. However, abortion became a widespread practice and, especially in urban areas, took the form of protest against the oppressive intrusion of state power into daily life (De Grazia 1993, p. 93). Alessandra Gissi, through in-depth archival research including documents from the judiciary and local authorities, has confirmed how during fascism abortion continued to exist, assisted by midwives who carried on procuring it and networks of women who made the practice possible, despite the emergence of a "culture of silence", imposed by fear of criminalisation, which was more organised that it had ever been in the past (Gissi 2006, pp. 83–84). As earlier noted by Passerini in research on abortion during fascism in Turin, the sheer necessity of abortion in the absence of other options seemed to instil an absence of guilt among women (Passerini in *Italia Contemporanea* 1983, p. 101).

Willson has contributed further to the question of women's responses to fascist policies, focusing on the role of propaganda. In a 2010 book translated into Italian a year later, she reflected on her earlier research arguing that fascist ideas about gender roles appeared widely in public discourse, in the press and on the radio, but, again, it is difficult to evaluate their impact. Educated middle-class women were more exposed to propaganda than industrial or rural workers, who happened to live in more remote places. Most importantly, the demographic campaign was a complete failure as the birth rate continued to fall and abortion remained a widespread practice; one reason was that the material and financial incentives were far too modest to compensate for the real costs involved in raising children (Willson 2011, p. 111; p. 118). At the same time, women continued to seek work, among the lower classes out of necessity and among the middle classes because many had received enough education to have social aspirations: on the whole, the story of women during fascism is one that challenges the idea of a mass consensus. This is because, as in the rest of Europe, modernising tendencies competed with the regime's ideology (Willson 2011, p. 136).

An important effort to analyse the history of women in contemporary Italy was published in 2022, edited by Silvia Salvatici with contributions from a number of historians who reflected on the latest interpretations and research in the field. Addressing the question of women's attitudes towards fascism, Paola Stelliferi noted that a number of Italian feminists had harboured some hopes about the new fascist movement, which had included female suffrage in its 1919 programme. As the repressive measures of the regime hit both women and men after 1925, women who wanted to maintain an active public role had to do so within a political framework focused on the nationalisation of the female masses, aimed at safeguarding women's reproductive role and their delegitimization in the workplace (Stelliferi in Salvatici 2022, p. 91). On the one hand, as Alessandra Pescarolo has shown, the regime produced laws for the support and well-being of pregnant workers and maternity benefits (excluding peasant women and domestic servants); on the other hand, the Gentile education reform prevented women from teaching specific subjects and sought to limit girls' enrolment in schools, reducing the number of women in secondary education. The other discrimination against women came with wage reductions (Pescarolo in Salvatici 2022, pp. 178–179). In the same volume, Elisabetta Vezzosi has underlined how, for ONMI, maternity was a social value and its task was therefore to construct "mother-citizens" together with other fascist organisations. She has also showed how the measures for supporting maternity and childhood ultimately did not develop into a permanent basis of assistance, but remained limited to emergency interventions. The funding for welfare was also limited for ONMI, and the material conditions of both rural and urban women did not improve significantly (Vezzosi in Salvatici 2022, p. 222).

The Catholic Church

As we have seen, discussions of totalitarianism and of the consensus also need to be concerned with the role of the catholic Church in Italy. In the post-war years, critical reflection on the responsibility of catholics for their support of the regime was avoided, while there was a tendency to underline the role of some catholics in the struggle against fascism. The catholic world had to legitimate itself within the new democratic framework. As Lucia Ceci has argued, it was mostly from the 1970s that new studies, in particular by Scoppola and Miccoli, began an investigation on the Roman Church's support for Mussolini, in order to understand whether and to what extent support was simply instrumental or more profound and substantial (Ceci in *Studi Storici* 2014, p. 123; p. 127). As early as the end of the 1970s, Isnenghi also highlighted how historiography on the catholic Church had hitherto avoided study on the mass nature of the new regime and any explanation of whether the Church competed with or allied with fascism. One consequence was the risk of "dignifying as anti-fascism what was in fact simply a struggle of competition", providing the Catholic hierarchy of the post-war period with the opportunity to "exhibit a non-existent anti-fascist virginity" (Isnenghi 1996, p. 143).

With the opening of the archives for the two pontificates of fascism, first that of Pius XI and recently of Pius XII, there has been new research in the twenty-first century, though it has not overturned the essential theses of earlier historiography. The connections between fascism and the Holy See have been recently studied by Ceci and Alberto Guasco, among others, who have demonstrated how these developed as early as 1919–1922, when the Vatican was forced to intervene to ask bishops and the clergy to remain outside a political struggle in which peasant catholic trade unions appeared to be moving towards collaboration with the socialist unions (Guasco 2013, p. 117). Ceci has showed how Mussolini played on the divisions within the catholic world, seeking an alliance with conservative catholics and the Vatican hierarchy and treating the PPI as a major enemy. Sturzo's attempt to keep the PPI on the side of democracy represented an obstacle for the affirmation of fascism. Mussolini was particularly worried that an alliance between the PPI and PSI could generate a government capable of restoring legality and stopping fascism. The *popolari* and Sturzo thus became his principal targets during the Facta governments of 1922. The decision taken at the PPI national congress in Turin in April 1923 to abandon support for the government turned the PPI into an open enemy and unleashed a new phase of fascist violence against the catholic associations (Ceci 2013, pp. 63–65; p. 87). At the same time, while in the provinces the fascist squads had unleashed violence against priests and the PPI headquarters, in Rome Mussolini turned his ecclesiastic policies upside down seeking an agreement with the Church (Guasco 2013, pp. 97–98). The divisions within the catholic world have also been an area of examination. In 1923 the Vatican daily, *L'Osservatore Romano*, cheered Giovanni Gentile's state education reform (Turi 1995, pp. 317–318). While fascists perpetrated violence against dioceses throughout Italy, the Vatican continued to express trust in Mussolini, since its priority was to solve the "Roman question" that had emerged when newly unified Italy in 1870 made Rome its capital, ending the temporal power of the popes (Ceci 2013, pp. 89–90).

Historians have continued to investigate the complex relationship of collaboration, suspicion, and competition between the Church and the regime as they battled for primacy in Italian society. Gabriele Rigano has shown how, for catholics, the Lateran pacts agreed in 1929 were not a final destination, but a point of departure in the attempt to catholicise fascism, while fascism intended to bend catholicism to its own national and imperialist needs (Rigano in Albanese 2021).

In conclusion, on the one hand, research from the 1990s up to the present has widened the themes and presented new interpretations of many aspects of the regime; on the other hand, twenty-first-century historians have continued to engage with traditional issues raised by the older historiography. As the next chapter will show, new research has also concentrated on fascism after the fall of Mussolini in 1943 and on the Italian Social Republic—the regime established by Mussolini during the German occupation of Italy, which lasted from September 1943 until April 1945, when the Allies and the Italian Resistance finally brought the Liberation of Italy and the end of the war.

References

Albanese, Giulia, *La marcia su Roma* (Rome-Bari: Laterza, 2006; English ed. 2019).
Albanese, Giulia (ed.), *Il fascismo italiano. Storia e interpretazioni* (Rome: Carocci, 2021; English ed. 2022).
Annali della Fondazione Luigi Micheletti, n. 5, *L'Italia in guerra, 1940–1943* (Brescia: Fondazione Luigi Micheletti, 1990–1991).

Baldoli, Claudia, *Exporting Fascism. Italian Fascists and Britain's Italians in the 1930s* (Oxford: Berg, 2003).
Baldoli, Claudia, Knapp, Andrew and Overy, Richard, *Bombing, States and Peoples in Western Europe, 1940–1945* (London: Continuum, 2011).
Ben-Ghiat, Ruth, *Fascist Modernities: Italy, 1922–1945* (Berkeley: University of California Press, 2001).
Berezin, Mabel, *Making the Fascist Self. The Political Culture of Interwar Italy* (Ithaca: Cornell University Press, 1997).
Bidussa, David, *Il mito del bravo italiano* (Milan: Il Saggiatore, 1994).
Canali, Mauro, *Il delitto Matteotti. Affarismo e politica nel primo governo Mussolini* (Bologna: Il Mulino, 1997).
Cavarocchi, Francesca, *Avanguardie dello spirito. Il fascismo e la propaganda culturale all'estero* (Rome: Carocci, 2010).
Ceci, Lucia, *L'interesse superiore. Il Vaticano e l'Italia di Mussolini* (Rome-Bari: Laterza, 2013; English ed. 2017).
Ceva, Lucio, *Storia delle forze armate in Italia* (Turin: UTET, 1999).
Colarizi, Simona, *L'Italia antifascista dal 1922 al 1940. La lotta dei protagonisti* (Rome-Bari: Laterza, 1976).
Colarizi, Simona, *L'opinione degli italiani sotto il regime, 1929–1943* (Rome-Bari: Laterza, 1991).
Colarizi, Simona, *Storia politica della Repubblica. Partiti, movimenti e istituzioni, 1943–2006* (Rome-Bari: Laterza, 2007).
Collotti, Enzo, *Fascismo e politica di potenza. Politica estera, 1922–1939*, with Nicola Labanca and Teodoro Sala (Florence: La Nuova Italia, 2000).
Collotti, Enzo, *Il fascismo e gli ebrei. La leggi razziali in Italia* (Rome-Bari: Laterza, 2006; 1st ed. 2003).
Corner, Paul, Galimi, Valeria, *Il fascismo in provincia. Articolazioni e gestione del potere tra centro e periferia* (Rome: Viella, 2014).
Corner, Paul, *The Fascist Party and Popular Opinion in Mussolini's Italy* (Oxford: Oxford University Press, 2012; Italian ed. 2015).
D'Alessandro, Leonardo Pompeo, *Giustizia fascista. Storia del tribunale speciale (1926–1943)* (Bologna: Il Mulino, 2020).
De Grazia, Victoria, *How Fascism ruled Women. Italy, 1922–1945* (Berkeley: University of California Press, 1992 Italian ed. 1993).
De Luna, Giovanni, *Donne in oggetto. L'antifascismo nella società italiana, 1922–1939* (Turin: Bollati Boringhieri, 1995).
De Luna, Giovanni (ed.), *Fascismo e storia d'Italia. A un secolo dalla marcia su Roma. Temi, narrazioni, fonti*, Annali Feltrinelli, n. 56 (Milan: Feltrinelli, 2022).
De Ninno, Fabio, *Fascisti sul mare. La Marina e gli ammiragli di Mussolini* (Rome-Bari: Laterza, 2017).
Di Figlia, Matteo, Farinacci. Il radicalismo fascista al potere (Rome: Donzelli, 2007).
Di Nolfo, Ennio, *Mussolini e la politica estera mussoliniana (1919–1933)* (Padua: Cedam, 1960).
Duggan, Christopher, *Fascist Voices. An Intimate History of Mussolini's Italy* (London: Vintage, 2012; Italian ed. 2013).
Duranti, Simone, *Leggi razziali fasciste e persecuzione antiebraica in Italia* (Milan: Unicopli, 2019).
Ebner, Michael R., *Ordinary Violence in Mussolini's Italy* (Cambridge: Cambridge University Press, 2011).

Ertola, Emanuele, *In terra d'Africa. Gli italiani che colonizzarono l'impero* (Rome-Bari: Laterza, 2017).
Fincardi, Marco, *Campagne emiliane in transizione* (Bologna: CLUEB, 2008).
Focardi, Filippo, *Il cattivo tedesco e il bravo italiano. La rimozione delle colpe della seconda guerra mondiale* (Rome-Bari: Laterza, 2013).
Fonzi, Paolo, *Fame di guerra. L'occupazione italiana della Grecia (1941–1943)* (Rome: Carocci, 2019).
Franzinelli, Mimmo, *Fascismo anno zero. 1919: la nascita dei fasci italiani di combattimento*, (Milan, Mondadori 2019).
Franzinelli, Mimmo, *L'insurrezione fascista. Storia e mito della Marcia su Roma* (Milan: Mondadori, 2022).
Gagliardi, Alessio, *Il corporativismo fascista* (Rome-Bari: Laterza, 2010).
Galimi, Valeria, *Sotto gli occhi di tutti. La società italiana e le persecuzioni contro gli ebrei* (Florence: Le Monnier, 2018).
Gallerano, Nicola, *L'uso pubblico della storia* (Milan: FrancoAngeli, 1995).
Gallerano, Nicola, "Critica e crisi del paradigma antifascista", in *Problemi del socialismo*, 1986, n. 7, pp. 106–133.
Gallerano, Nicola, "Le ricerche locali sul fascismo", in *Italia Contemporanea*, 1991, n. 184, pp. 388–397.
Gentile, Emilio, *Il mito dello Stato nuovo* (Rome-Bari: Laterza, 1999; 1st ed. 1982).
Gentile, Emilio, *Fascismo. Storia e interpretazione* (Rome-Bari: Laterza, 2002).
Gentile, Emilio, Di Scala, Spencer M. (eds), *Mussolini socialista* (Rome-Bari: Laterza, 2015).
Gibelli, Antonio, *L'officina della guerra: la grande guerra e le trasformazioni del mondo mentale* (Turin: Bollati Boringhieri, 1991).
Gissi, Alessandra, *Le segrete manovre delle donne* (Rome: Biblink, 2006).
Granata, Ivano, *Milano rossa. Ascesa e declino del socialismo (1919–1926)* (Milan: Mimesis, 2018).
Guasco, Alberto, *Cattolici e fascisti. La Santa sede e la politica italiana all'alba del regime: 1919–1925* (Bologna: Il Mulino, 2013).
Ignazi, Piero, *I partiti in Italia dal 1945 al 2018* (Bologna: Il Mulino, 2018).
Isnenghi, Mario, *Il mito della grande guerra* (Bologna: Il Mulino, 2007; 1st ed. 1970).
Isnenghi, Mario, *Le guerre degli italiani. Parole, immagini, ricordi, 1848–1945* (Milan: Mondadori, 1989).
Isnenghi, Mario, *L'Italia del fascio* (Florence: Giunti, 1996).
Isnenghi, Mario, Ceschin, Daniele (eds), *Gli italiani in guerra: conflitti, identità, memorie dal Risorgimento ai nostri giorni*, vol. 3.1, *La grande guerra: dall'intervento alla "vittoria mutilata"* (Turin: UTET, 2008).
Isnenghi, Mario, *Storia d'Italia. I fatti e le percezioni dal Risorgimento alla società dello spettacolo* (Rome-Bari: Laterza, 2011a).
Isnenghi, Mario, *Dieci lezioni sull'Italia contemporanea* (Rome: Donzelli, 2011b).
Journal of Modern Italian Studies, n. 5, 2014: *Two new books on Fascism. A review, the authors' responses and the reviewer's comments*, pp. 665–683.
Knox, MacGregor, Alleati di Hitler. Le regie forze armate, il regime fascista e la guerra del 1940–1943 (Milan: Garzanti, 2002; English ed. 2000).
Knox, MacGregor, "I testi 'aggiustati' dei discorsi segreti di Grandi", in P*assato e presente*, n. 13, 1987, pp. 97-117.
Labanca, Nicola, *Oltremare. Storia dell'espansione coloniale italiana* (Bologna: Il Mulino, 2002).

Labanca, Nicola, *Una guerra per l'Impero. Memorie della campagna d'Etiopia: 1935–36* (Bologna: Il Mulino, 2005).
Labanca, Nicola, *La guerra italiana per la Libia, 1911–1931* (Bologna: Il Mulino, 2012).
Leed, Eric, *No Man's Land. Combat and identity in World War 1* (Cambridge: Cambridge University Press, 1979).
Levis Sullam, Simon, *L'apostolo a brandelli. L'eredità di Mazzini tra Risorgimento e fascismo* (Rome-Bari: Laterza, 2010).
Lupo, Salvatore, *Il fascismo. La politica in un regime totalitario* (Rome: Donzelli, 2000).
Luzzatto, Sergio, *Il corpo del duce. Un cadavere tra immaginazione, storia e memoria* (Turin: Einaudi, 1998).
Luzzatto, Sergio, *La strada per Addis Abeba. Lettere di un camionista dell'Impero (1936–1941)* (Turin: Paravia, 2000).
Luzzatto, Sergio, *La crisi dell'antifascismo* (Turin: Einaudi, 2004).
Memoria e Ricerca, n. 2, 2021: Special issue on *Leader carismatici e movimenti sociali nell'Ottocento europeo*, ed. by Marco Manfredi and Elena Papadia.
Milza, Pierre, *Mussolini* (Rome: Carocci, 2000; French ed. 1999).
Minesso, Michela, *Madri figli welfare. Istituzioni e politiche dall'Italia liberale ai giorni nostri* (Bologna: Il Mulino, 2015).
Mondini, Marco, *Roma 1922. Il fascismo e la guerra mai finita* (Bologna: Il Mulino, 2022).
Mosse, George L., *Fallen Soldiers. Reshaping the Memory of the World Wars* (Oxford: Oxford University Press, 1990).
Osti Guerrazzi, Amedeo, *Esercito italiano in Slovenia, 1941–1943. Strategie di repressione antipartigiana* (Rome: Viella, 2011).
Paci, Deborah, *Corsica fatal, Malta baluardo di romanità. L'irredentismo fascista nel mare nostrum (1922–1942)* (Florence: Le Monnier, 2015).
Papadia, Elena, *La forza dei sentimenti. Anarchici e socialisti in Italia (1870-1900)* (Bologna: Il Mulino, 2019).
Passerini, Luisa, "Donne operaie e aborto nella Torino fascista", in *Italia Contemporanea*, n. 151–152, 1983, pp. 83–109.
Passerini, Luisa, *Torino operaia e fascismo* (Rome-Bari: Laterza, 1984; English ed. 1987).
Passerini, Luisa, *Mussolini immaginario. Storia di una biografia 1915–1939* (Rome-Bari: Laterza, 1991).
Pes, Alessandro, *La costruzione dell'impero fascista. Politiche di regime per una società coloniale* (Rome: Aracne, 2010).
Petri, Rolf, *Storia economica d'Italia. Dalla Grande guerra al miracolo economico: 1918–1963* (Bologna: Il Mulino, 2002).
Poesio, Camilla, *Il confino fascista. L'arma silenziosa del regime* (Rome-Bari: Laterza, 2011).
Pretelli, Matteo, *Il fascismo e gli italiani all'estero* (Bologna: Clueb, 2010).
Quazza, Guido, *Fascismo e società italiana* (Turin: Einaudi, 1973).
Ridolfi, Maurizio, *Storia dei partiti politici. L'Italia dal Risorgimento alla Repubblica* (Milan: Bruno Mondadori, 2008).
Rochat, Giorgio, *Le guerre italiane 1935–1943. Dall'impero d'Etiopia alla disfatta* (Turin: Einaudi, 2008).
Rodogno, Davide, *Il nuovo ordine mediterraneo. Le politiche di occupazione dell'Italia fascista in Europa, 1940–1943* (Turin: Bollati Boringhieri, 2003; English ed. 2006).
Rodrigo, Javier, "A fascist warfare? Italian fascism and war experience in the Spanish Civil War (1936–39)", in *War in History*, n. 26, 2019, pp. 86–104.

Sabbatucci, Giovanni, Vidotto, Vittorio, *Storia d'Italia* (6 vols), vol. 4: *Guerre e fascismo 1914–1943* (Rome-Bari: Laterza, 1995–1999).

Salvati, Mariuccia, *Il regime e gli impiegati* (Rome-Bari: Laterza, 1992).

Salvati, Mariuccia, "Lo Stato sociale in Italia: Caratteri originali e motivi di una crisi", in *Passato e presente*, n. 32, 1994, pp. 15–18.

Salvatici, Silvia (ed.), *Storia delle donne nell'Italia contemporanea* (Rome: Carocci, 2022).

Salvatori, Paola S. (ed.), *Il fascismo e la storia* (Pisa: Edizioni della Normale, 2020).

Santomassimo, Pasquale, "Il ruolo di Renzo De Felice", in *Italia Contemporanea*, n. 212, 1998, pp. 555–563.

Sarfatti, Michele, *Mussolini contro gli ebrei. Cronaca dell'elaborazione delle leggi del 1938* (Torino: Zamorani, 1994).

Segreto, Luciano, *Marte e Mercurio. Industria bellica e sviluppo economico in Italia, 1861–1940* (Milan: FrancoAngeli, 1997).

Simonelli, Federico Carlo, *D'Annunzio e il mito di Fiume. Riti, simboli, narrazioni* (Pisa: Pacini, 2021).

Sternhell, Zeev, *Naissance de l'idéologie fasciste* (Paris: Fayard, 1989; Italian ed. 1993; English ed. 1994).

Snodi. Pubblici e privati nella storia contemporanea, n. 1, 2007: special issue on *Rotte dell'io/rotte del noi*.

Studi Storici, n. 1, 2014: special issue on *Fascismo: Itinerari storiografici da un secolo all'altro*.

Toniolo, Gianni, *L'economia dell'Italia fascista* (Rome-Bari: Laterza, 1980).

Tranfaglia, Nicola, *La prima guerra mondiale e il fascismo* (Turin: UTET, 1995).

Troilo, Simona, *Pietre d'oltremare. Scavare, conservare, immaginare l'Impero (1899–1940)* (Rome-Bari: Laterza, 2021).

Turi, Gabriele, *Giovanni Gentile. Una biografia* (Florence: Giunti, 1995).

Ventrone, Angelo, *La seduzione totalitaria. Guerra, modernità, violenza politica (1914–1918)* (Rome: Donzelli, 2003).

Ventura, Andrea, *Il diciannovismo fascista. Un mito che non passa* (Rome: Viella, 2021).

Vivarelli, Roberto, *Storia delle origini del fascismo. L'Italia dalla grande guerra alla marcia su Roma*, 3 vols (Bologna: Il Mulino, 1991).

Willson, Perry, *Peasant Women and Politics in Fascist Italy: The Massaie Rurali* (London: Routledge, 2002).

Willson, Perry, Italiane. Biografia del Novecento (Rome-Bari: Laterza, 2011; English ed. 2010).

CHAPTER 5

The Italian Social Republic (1943–1945): Historiography on Fascism's Final Years

The Italian Social Republic (*Repubblica Sociale Italiana*—RSI) was a product of the regime's military defeat and the German occupation of Italy following the September 1943 armistice. Mussolini's regime ended in July 1943, precipitated by the Allied landing on Sicily. On 25 July, with the war almost lost, the king—for the first time since the march on Rome—decided to act against Mussolini after the fascist Grand Council had voted in favour of Mussolini's dismissal. The *duce* was arrested and marshal Badoglio became the new prime minister. Mussolini's was a silent fall, imposed from above, but it was immediately welcomed from below: as the radio announced the news, the summer evening saw massive crowds in the streets and piazzas, cheering and shouting that the war and fascism were over. Although the radio made clear that the war would continue, the population could not see any reason to go on fighting once the regime had fallen. However, as a famous partisan song from Piedmont (entitled *Badoglieide*) reminded people, Badoglio represented continuity rather than break: "made fat by fascism", responsible for the war in Ethiopia, for the shameful aggression against France, and, finally, for having left the fascists in power and put anti-fascists in prison—"the shirt was no longer black/but fascism remained in power".

There was as a result a mass reaction against the symbols of the dictatorship: statues of Mussolini were taken down, images of Roman lictors on public buildings destroyed and streets renamed; the enraged population needed to reject an entire age, to leave the past and part of themselves behind—since most people had been, or had behaved as fascists under the regime. In the meantime, secret bargaining between the Allies and Badoglio led to the declaration of an armistice on 8 September, and the Germans suddenly became the enemy. Again, the popular reaction was a delighted belief that the war was really over. The army collapsed and everyone escaped who could, starting with the king and Badoglio who abandoned Rome to German vengeance and

© The Author(s), under exclusive license to Springer Nature Switzerland AG 2023
C. Baldoli, *Italian Fascism, 1914-1945*,
https://doi.org/10.1007/978-3-031-41904-1_5

sought refuge in Allied-liberated Southern Italy. Soldiers left the field without orders, pursuing what seemed the only sensible idea: to go home—the title of a famous film made later in 1961, *Tutti a casa* by Luigi Comencini. The partisan Beppe Fenoglio (author of the well-known novel *Johnny the Partisan*), related in *Primavera di bellezza* [Spring of beauty] of the shock with which a group of soldiers greeted the news, and the perception that an army in Italy no longer existed (Fenoglio 1991, p. 107). It was difficult to cross Italy and escape from the Germans; some 600,000 Italian soldiers were deported to German internment camps. Women took on a major role of defending, feeding and helping Italian and Allied soldiers, demonstrating that, despite the lack of a state to give orders, civil society continued to function, and a country named Italy still existed.

Which Italy, however? Fascist Italy had died and the army and the state had collapsed. Some historians have claimed that 8 September represented the "death of the fatherland" (Galli della Loggia 1996). This was certainly the way that fascists felt: one of them, the young Carlo Mazzantini, expressed these feelings in his wartime memoir *A cercar la bella morte* [Looking for the beautiful death]: "There was no more Italy; there was no more government, no more army. … Italy had become nothing more than a territory with a population occupied by a foreign army" (Mazzantini 1995, p. 21). The population sought ways to survive hunger and the bombing and waited for the end of the war, welcoming the Allies as liberators as they progressed from southern to northern Italy. Such attitudes expressed weariness and opportunism, but also the attraction of the myth of America—the rich country whither many Italians had emigrated—symbolised during those months by soldiers bringing food, cigarettes and chocolate. For many Italians, these were products from a world of consumption they had admired in the Hollywood movies that had still been permissible to watch under the regime.

The death of the old *patria* corresponded to the birth of two new opposed ones: on 12 September Mussolini was rescued by the Germans and established a fascist republic, the RSI, controlled by Nazi Germany between the west of Lake Garda and Venice (also named the "Salò Republic" due to the geographical location of a large number of the new ministries); the other Italy was born in the mountains where partisan groups organised to fight fascism and Nazism and were victorious, alongside the Allies, in April 1945. It was for this reason that the Italian republic founded in 1946, after a referendum abolished the monarchy, could declare itself "born of the Resistance". The names partisans chose for their armed groups were those of the heroes of the struggle for the unification of Italy in the nineteenth century (Garibaldi, Mazzini, Goffredo Mameli) and heroes of anti-fascist martyrdom like Matteotti, Gramsci and Rosselli. Facing the partisan brigades, the RSI fought a ferocious and increasingly unsuccessful war between 1943 and 1945, a civil war that was part of the wider war of liberation fought between the Allies and the Germans on Italian soil.

A "Civil War"

However, it took many decades for the historiography to acknowledge the existence of a civil war in Italy in 1943–1945. After the war, the concept was only utilised by the defeated fascists, who claimed that it was a civil war as a way of obtaining political recognition: if the war fought in Italy in 1943–1945 was simply a war of liberation, it involved the Germans on one side, and the Allies, with the help of the Resistance, on the other, but not the fascists still loyal to Mussolini. To argue that it was a civil war, a war between Italians, meant applying the status of combatants to the fascists enrolled in the RSI, an argument developed in a three-volume work by neo-fascist journalist Giorgio Pisanò (Pisanò 1965–1966). The former partisans always denied the fascists such status, claiming that they had simply played a role subordinate to the German command.

A lively historiographical debate began to emerge on the fortieth anniversary of Italy's liberation in 1985. In that year, historian Claudio Pavone published an article in *Italia Contemporanea* based on a paper he had presented at an international conference in the same year in Milan on the theme "Italy in the Second World War and in the Resistance". The conference strongly underlined the need to propose new research and interpretations on the war of liberation of 1943–1945. Pavone explored the choices, the dilemmas and the existential dimension of the situation that evolved from the armistice of September 1943, posing the question of what it meant for a population to find itself in the middle of a war fought by two foreign armies in a context of "civil war", in a country divided in territorial, institutional, and social terms (Pavone in *Italia Contemporanea* 1985; Cooke in *Italia contemporanea*, 2022).

However, it was during another conference (on the RSI) the same year, organised by the Foundation Luigi Micheletti in Brescia, that Pavone's reference to the civil war caused controversy, particularly provoking protest from communist party leader Giancarlo Pajetta. Pavone observed a widespread difficulty for people to accept that the RSI, too, stood "within the history of our country" and that Italian fascists, "against whom Italian antifascists fought", were not "ghosts born of hell": on the contrary, they were "hated precisely because they were themselves Italian" (Pavone in *Annali* 1986, p. 396). Moreover, what he defined as a civil war between fascists and anti-fascists could be considered as a sort of day of reckoning in a struggle that had begun in 1919–1922 (although he did not use the words "civil war" for the 1919–1922 period). The Resistance, Pavone argued, wanted its final confrontation to be against fascism, against a native force that had been able to achieve and manage power well before the arrival of German tanks—unlike the situation facing the resistance in France (Pavone in *Annali* 1986, pp. 398–399).

Some historians had already argued that for the fascists the confrontation of 1943–1945 was a civil war, as shown, for example, in one of the first important reconstructions of RSI history, written by Frederick W. Deakin in 1962 and translated into Italian the following year. According to Deakin, the fascists were clear on the designation "civil war" as they met in Verona to draft the Republic's constitution in November 1943 (Deakin 1963, p. 839); an awareness that was confirmed in July 1944 with the creation of the voluntary militia of the Black Brigades—according to Pavone, a landmark moment in the fascist commitment to the civil war. The conflict was, according to the militia's founder and Republican Fascist Party secretary Alessandro Pavolini, a contest between "politicians in arms against politicians in arms". The perception from the antifascist side was more complex, as civil and patriotic wars were intertwined (Pavone in *Annali* 1986, pp. 403–405). During the conference debate Pajetta rejected the definition entirely: "it was not a civil war, it was a people's war, a unitary war, a war for independence". The unitary aspect of antifascism and its identification with the entire Italian people in 1943–1945 (in this light, Italian fascists were simply servants of the Germans) implied that fascism had been a mass dictatorship, but one based solely on a passive consensus (Pajetta in *Annali* 1986, p. 431).

The historiographical debate generated by the Brescia conference was followed by publicity in the media that was unusual for an academic initiative. In 1985, Pavone began to introduce his concept of three wars that overlapped and connected with each other in 1943–1945: a patriotic war of liberation fought by the Resistance alongside the Allies against Nazi Germany; a civil war between Italian fascists and antifascist partisans in the RSI territory; and a class war represented by the participation of the working class in the insurrection, bringing together the political and economic struggle.

Another conference held in Belluno three years later showed (even from the title: "Resistance: war, war of liberation, civil war") that many historians now shared Pavone's interpretation. On that occasion, Pavone drew attention to two important issues: first, that the definition of civil war did not imply any comparison between fascists and antifascist partisans; on the contrary, he argued, it was especially in civil wars that contrary positions were completely defined; second, that it was not possible to remove the fascists of the RSI from Italy's history, just as it was not possible to remove from it racism and antisemitism, for to do so would have meant to "indulge in the bad (and catholic) Italian habit of an easy self-forgiveness" (Pavone in Legnani and Vendramini 1990, p. 32). In 1991 he finally published a monumental work of scholarship, matured after decades of labour in the archives, under the title *A Civil War*. The book, translated into English in 2013, dealt not only with the war between Italians, but with all three types of conflict that Pavone had identified (Pavone 1991).

THE RSI AS PART OF THE HISTORY OF ITALIAN FASCISM

Was the RSI a "new" form of fascism? Can it be considered a form of "neofascism", somehow detached from the fascist regime of 1922–1943? What distinguished the RSI from the previous regime was undoubtedly that its history developed alongside German occupation. At the same time, it was not simply a history of collaboration with the occupiers, which was common to all the countries occupied by Nazi Germany, because of the presence of an indigenous fascist regime run by Italians, who had already taken part in the regime that had governed Italy for the previous 20 years. It is thus necessary to include the RSI in the wider history of Italian fascism as it was in many ways a development of fascism within the new conditions of war and occupation. Moreover, the occupier was an ally—the ally that Mussolini had chosen from at least 1936.

Despite providing a generally negative view of the RSI and of its impact on the Italian population, in his last volume of Mussolini's biography (which was left incomplete and published posthumously), De Felice supported an idea that was widely popular in the apologetic post-war literature of the RSI: that Mussolini, old and tired, agreed against his own will to lead the fascist republic because he was forced to do so by the Germans, and in order to avoid a much worse fate for the Italian population under Nazi occupation. Apart from owing his freedom and possibly his life to Hitler, De Felice argued, Mussolini was moved by "patriotic reason", a true "sacrifice" for Italy's sake. Only in this way could he prevent Hitler from transforming Italy into a "new Poland" and make "the occupation regime less heavy and tragic"; furthermore, in case of victory, Germany would have to take into account Italy's loyalty (De Felice 1995, pp. 114–115; De Felice 1997, pp. 64–71).

However, De Felice did not provide any historical evidence for such conclusions, apart from later testimonies from Mussolini's son Vittorio and other fascists, documents characterised by uncertain authenticity. The lack of grounded historical research behind the thesis did not prevent it being publicised and accepted at the level of a public opinion that was inclined to blame every tragedy on Nazi Germany and to believe in the idea of a benevolent Mussolini. In fact, historians both before and after De Felice provided accurate accounts, based on a wealth of archival research, that completely overturn that picture. In 1993 Lutz Klinkhammer published a monumental history of the German occupation of Italy, based on both Italian and German archival sources. Klinkhammer demonstrated the importance of the RSI for Germany: as soon as Italy withdrew from the war, the moment had come for the Germans to fully exploit Italy's economic resources, including its workforce—a project already started in 1940, given Italy's dependence on the stronger ally. Hitler's decision to support fascism and treat Italy as an "ally", continuing the situation of the Axis and the Pact of Steel, allowed him to demonstrate the existence of a collaborationist regime internationally as well as ensuring the functioning of the civil administration and public order, and the structuring of the occupation regime (Klinkhammer 1993, pp. 413–416). As Monica Fioravanzo has noted, these facts counter the idea that Hitler could have planned a Polish-style occupation of Italy. Indeed, the alleged German threat of treating Italy like Poland was a recurrent discourse in post-war fascist memorialisation that intended to justify the RSI, but does not appear in any German document. Moreover, Italian documents demonstrate that Mussolini had no intention of renouncing fascist rule again, and was willing to reconstruct a new fascist government on the side of Nazi Germany. His withdrawal from the political scene would have meant abandoning fascism, while at the same time acknowledging his own failure and the failure of the movement (Fioravanzo 2009, p. 13; p. 49).

Building on important work by Luigi Ganapini (1999), Dianella Gagliani focused on the militarisation of the Republican Fascist Party, showing Mussolini's personal responsibility for the formation of the Black Brigades in June 1944, the most brutal and violent RSI organisation employed against the partisans. This decision challenges the idea of the RSI as a government of national defence against German power, and shows the continuities between the history of fascism up to July 1943 and the later 20 months of the republic. What emerged in September 1943 were not forces that had remained marginal for a long time, but instead, in Gagliani's words, "a subject that had dominated the public space for two decades, having being invented and having found its success for the first time in Italy, that is to say fascism" (Gagliani 2017, p. 6).

The history of Milan during the RSI is a fitting example, as a recent account by Marco Cuzzi shows, because the fall of the regime increased among the most radical elements of fascism the will to avenge the overthrow of Mussolini. They aimed to "return to the origins" through an anti-capitalist, anti-Semitic and corporative ideology. However, these were not new men, but "old ones" (Cuzzi 2022, p. 36; p. 42). For Ganapini, too, there were continuities with the previous regime, though there was also an attempt to renew the fascist experience through building a new order that could be linked more closely to the model of Nazi totalitarianism. Perhaps the most distinctive aspect of RSI propaganda was the accent on "socialisation", a (failed) attempt to attract the working class against the forces of capitalism, which had allegedly betrayed fascism by siding with the Allies. The RSI now proposed an authoritarian and totalitarian order identified with state institutions and the fascist party. Not only had the industrialists and the monarchy abandoned fascism, but the Vatican also refused to officially recognise the RSI, while the Church—a fundamental ally during the regime—did not provide any support for Mussolini. Despite the difficulty of collaborating with the powerful German ally-occupier, the new regime tried to identify with the idea of a European order that could be shared with Nazi Germany, aspirations that existed before 1943, and were thus "not external to the history of Italy" (Ganapini 1999, pp. 13–17).

The other controversial theme concerns the collaboration of the fascist republic in the Holocaust. Anti-Semitism was incorporated into the republic's constitution, the *Carta di Verona*, a sort of manifesto without juridical value, but the basis for the administrative application of anti-Jewish policies. In this way, anti-Semitism continued to be applied as it had been during the fascist regime, following the racist laws of 1938. From early January 1944, a decree established the right to confiscate all Jewish goods. As early as December 1943 the republic's police headquarters had begun a hunt for Jews, arresting and interning people of Jewish origin: this was carried out according to norms promulgated by the Italian interior ministry, independent from the Nazi occupiers, through a pre-existing organisation and five years of experience of discrimination and persecution. What was different from the previous regime was the participation in the "final solution". The republican police and the fascist militia arrested Jewish men, women, and children and interned them in local concentration camps, for transfer to the national camp at Fossoli in Emilia and, from August 1944, to Gries near Bolzano, as well as other camps in Verona and the Risiera di San Sabba near Trieste (the only Italian camp with a cremation oven). From these camps Jews were handed over to the Germans and sent to extermination camps such as Auschwitz-Birkenau (Fioravanzo 2009, pp. 91–97). There were thus elements of continuity with the fascist regime, but also a move from persecution to genocide (as detailed in Sarfatti 1994), in active collaboration with the Nazi ally.

From the 1980s onwards, historians have thus established a discourse on the RSI based on thorough scholarly research, and without any attempt to justify it by blaming the violence of the civil war on the Germans, or to provide opportunities for treating the RSI ahistorically. The historians who have taken part in the debate on the RSI, by inserting it firmly within the history of Italian fascism, have contributed to the essential attempt to confront the entire fascist past. This is still an open debate in Italian public opinion.

References

Annali della Fondazione Luigi Micheletti, 2, *La Repubblica Sociale Italiana, 1943–1945* (Brescia: Fondazione Luigi Micheletti, 1986).
Cuzzi, Marco, *Seicento giorni di terrore a Milano. Vita quotidiana ai tempi di Salò* (Vicenza: Neri Pozza, 2022).
Deakin, Frederick W., *Storia della repubblica di Salò*, 2 vols (Turin: Einaudi, 1963; English ed. 1962).
De Felice, Renzo, *Rosso e nero*, ed. by Pasquale Chessa (Milan: Baldini & Castoldi, 1995).
De Felice, Renzo, *Mussolini l'alleato. La guerra civile, 1943–1945* (Turin: Einaudi, 1997).
Fenoglio, Beppe, *Primavera di bellezza* (Milan: Garzanti, 1991; 1st ed. 1959).
Fioravanzo, Monica, *Mussolini e Hitler. La Repubblica sociale sotto il Terzo Reich* (Rome: Donzelli, 2009).
Gagliani, Dianella, *Brigate nere. Mussolini e la militarizzazione del Partito fascista repubblicano* (Turin: Bollati Boringhieri, 2017; 1st ed. 1999).
Galli Della Loggia, Ernesto, *La morte della patria. La crisi dell'idea di nazione tra Resistenza, antifascismo e Repubblica* (Rome-Bari: Laterza, 1996).
Ganapini, Luigi, *La repubblica delle camicie nere* (Milan: Garzanti, 1999).
Klinkhammer, Lutz, *L'occupazione tedesca in Italia, 1943–1945* (Turin: Bollati Boringhieri, 1993).
Legnani, Massimo, Vendramini, Ferruccio (eds), *Guerra, guerra di liberazione, guerra civile* (Milan: FrancoAngeli, 1990).
Mazzantini, Carlo, *A cercar la bella morte* (Venice: Marsilio, 1995; 1st ed. 1986).
Pavone, Claudio, "Tre governi e due occupazioni", in *Italia Contemporanea*, n. 160, 1985 (and comment on this article by Philip Cooke in *Italia Contemporanea*, n. 300, 2022).
Pavone, Claudio, *Una guerra civile. Saggio storico sulla moralità nella Resistenza* (Turin: Bollati Boringhieri, 1991; English ed. 2013).
Pisanò, Giorgio, *Storia della guerra civile in Italia (1943–1945)* (Milan: Edizioni FPE, 1965–1966).
Sarfatti, Michele, *Mussolini contro gli ebrei. Cronaca dell'elaborazione delle leggi del 1938* (Turin: Zamorani, 1994).

CHAPTER 6

Conclusion

Aurora Rossoni, my grandmother, was born in Treviglio in 1916 and worked in a textile factory near Milan from 1932 to 1942. As a small child in the post-war years, she once hid under a table, terrified to see a fascist squad hitting her uncle. She was a young woman in the 1930s, when the fascist regime achieved, according to many historians, the peak of its consensus. However, as she told me when I interviewed her in the 1990s, there was no perception of fascism among the women who worked in the factory, as no one talked about politics: "the girls were not suited to fascism, nor to the new age". In 1940, Mussolini visited the factory, but did not talk about the war. She was chosen as the girl who had to present Mussolini with a bunch of flowers and welcome him with the roman salute. The *duce* caressed her head and said that all the girls had been very good. After that he went to address a completely crowded cathedral square in Milan, where he delivered a belligerent speech about the war to general applause.

It is by studying the countless lives of women and men of the interwar period that historians, through oral interviews, diaries, correspondences and memoirs, as well as fascist reports (by both fascist police and local authorities), have tackled the question of the consensus, perhaps one of the most debated issues from the 1970s until today. In his visits to factories such as Fiat Mirafiori in Turin and Breda in Milan, Mussolini was met with a silence that contrasted with the acclamation he received in the town squares. As the story of Aurora Rossoni confirms, large parts of the working class remained impenetrable to fascism. This has been supported by much of the scholarly research, which demonstrated that consensus for fascism came mostly from the middle classes. Even in that case, as we have seen in the previous chapters, it is necessary to distinguish between active and passive consensus, specific periods of the regime, and different parts of Italy. In the Second World War, Italians in air raid shelters were cursing Mussolini in industrial cities, but praying for him in small towns in the areas bordering with Austria. Consensus is an evanescent concept that is

© The Author(s), under exclusive license to Springer Nature Switzerland AG 2023
C. Baldoli, *Italian Fascism, 1914-1945*,
https://doi.org/10.1007/978-3-031-41904-1_6

difficult to gauge—with the obvious but important consideration that consensus in a dictatorship is different from consensus in a democracy. Historians have engaged with De Felice's idea of consensus from the 1970s, overcoming the previous picture of a dictatorship only based on repression and violence, but they have done so by producing a more complex and nuanced picture.

As I was writing this book, I took part in many events for the centenary of the march on Rome, which provided me with opportunities for an appraisal of the current historiographical debate on Italian fascism. The multifaceted issue of consensus was only one of the questions that resurfaced in the discussions of the centenary. As a conclusion to this overview of the historiography of Italian fascism, I seek to single out other themes that I found most stimulating in that debate. One of them is the question of whether there was an Italian "civil war" in the interwar period, which connects with the wider historiography on the concept of a "European civil war" (Traverso 2007). Was there a link between the "civil war" in 1919–1922 and 1943–1945? As explained by Luca Baldissara at a conference organised by the Gramsci Foundation in Rome in October 2022, it is difficult to extend the concept of civil war to 1919–1922: following the "red biennial" no revolutionary project developed, but instead the workers' movement focused on defending itself against fascism: if anything, it was a one-way civil war, in which only one side was armed. Fascism conquered power without the need to fight a civil war, thanks to the acquiescence of the liberal ruling class. From that point of view, and thanks to extensive research on fascist violence and its supporters among the ruling class, the fascist seizure of power appears closer to a preventive counter-revolution than to a civil war.

Even the ousting from power of Mussolini on 25 July took place without violence; the RSI, however, changed the perspective. For Hitler, the RSI was fundamental because it confirmed the tenure of fascism at a European level, and helped to maintain a southern front in his war against the Allies; but the control of territory against antifascist partisans was led by Italian fascists. This is when the civil war was evident, a war between Italians that assumed the traits of a vendetta, for example when partisans were tortured and killed in front of their families, who were forced to watch the gory spectacle. This type of violence was conducted by Italians, it was a brutality that rested on mutual acquaintance, a form of fratricidal violence (Ranzato 1994). Moreover, the antifascist violence against fascists can be seen as a payback for the fascist violence since 1919–1922.

One of the areas that showed much progress in the recent historiography, as evident in some of the centenary initiatives, is the subject of the fascist wars and the links between war and colonialism throughout the whole life of the regime. Born of the First World War, the regime continuously talked about war and provoked military conflicts for much of its existence, ending with participation and defeat in the Second World War. Historians have begun to study the Italian occupations from the mid-1930s by taking seriously the fascist project of territorial expansion and fascist totalitarianism, despite its failure. Mussolini's plan for a new Mediterranean order demonstrated that fascist occupations during the Second World War were not simply appendixes to the Nazi occupations. The wars of the regime are specifically defined as fascist conflicts, particularly the Ethiopian war, which had a clear ideological purpose and involved the fascist militia as fighters: it was not so much a colonial war, a view also underlined by Ethiopian historiography, as it was a conflict between two sovereign states (Zewde 1991; Teshale 1995). It involved a mobilisation unprecedented in Italian history: a problem for fascism was the lack of colonial consciousness and culture of the Italians, so it was necessary to mark a quantitative and qualitative change with liberal Italy. The idea of fascist modernity found justification in the colonial reality, not only in military terms, but also in the imagery of the Italian cities and architecture in the colonies.

The contribution of architects to the totalitarian shift of the 1930 also received attention in 2022, in connection with the difficult question of fascist heritage and of the relationship between Italians and the many sites of the fascist past today—monuments and buildings still standing in every Italian city. In Rome, for example, the traces of the regime are de-politicised as they integrate with the ancient urban landscape; across Italy, mausoleums to prominent fascists are neither restored nor demolished, as an expression of the indifference of local administrations to history and a general will to forget. In the same way, the numerous *fasci* headquarters dispersed in the Italian provinces are not historically contextualised. As a result, the general attitude of the population is one of local pride for a generic architectural heritage, without any knowledge of the history of the regime that produced it (Albanese and Ceci 2022).

The indifference towards the material legacy of fascism has thus raised the question—from which this book started—as to whether Italians have yet confronted their fascist past. In one of the many conferences organised in 2022, by the Foundation Clementina Calzari Trebeschi in Brescia (named after a teacher who died, with seven other victims, because of a neo-fascist bomb in that city in 1974), Focardi highlighted some historical reasons behind the difficulty Italians have in coming to terms with the results of historiography. He mentioned the Crocean idea of fascism as a parenthesis, which, as we have seen, presented the fascists as external to Italy's history. According to that interpretation, Italy's progressive history and tradition meant that there were enough antibodies in Italian society against fascism to prevent it becoming as violent as Nazism. Young people, for example, were indoctrinated, but only superficially. This concept was widely disseminated (not only within liberal milieus) and it implied that fascist Italy was somehow against nature, while Nazi Germany was according to nature: Italians only acted as fascists, while Germans really were Nazis. The communist party leader Togliatti had sustained in similar terms the argument that fascism did not penetrate the soul of Italian society, thanks to the democratic traditions of the Risorgimento and to socialism. All these beliefs permeated the post-war narrative, where Hitler was portrayed as a demon and Mussolini as a bogus dictator. The theses by De Felice, which partly supported these views, were relaunched in the media by right-wing journalists. The "retroactive defascistisation" of fascism, as Emilio Gentile defined it in 2002, began immediately after the end of the war, and is still occurring in Italy. Fascism was deprived of its criminal and repressive characteristics and turned in something that was not fascism, now stripped of its totalitarian character. The reference to Nazi Germany as a negative model helped the construction of what Bidussa (1996, p. 75) has called the "demon of analogy": he argued that while it was correct to draw comparisons in the work of historians, the result at the level of public opinion was not a scientific explanation, but the construction of a deceptive image of the fascist regime still prevalent today.

REFERENCES

Albanese, Giulia, Ceci, Lucia (eds), *I luoghi del fascismo. Memoria, politica, rimozione* (Rome: Viella, 2022).

Bidussa, David, *Il mito del bravo italiano* (Milan: Il Saggiatore, 1996).

Ranzato, Gabriele, *Guerre fratricide. Le guerre civili in età contemporanea* (Turin: Bollati Boringhieri, 1994).

Teshale, Tibebu, *The Making of Modern Ethiopia, 1896–1974* (Lawrenceville, N.J.: Red Sea Press, 1995).

Traverso, Enzo, *A ferro e fuoco. La guerra civile europea, 1914–1945* (Bologna: Il Mulino, 2007).

Zewde, Barhu, *A History of Modern Ethiopia, 1855–1974* (London: J. Currey, 1991).

Index

A
Abruzzo, 28
Action Party (*Partito d'Azione*, PdA), 40
Africa, 57, 81, 83, 84
Air raid shelters, 111
Albanese, Giulia, 2, 12, 66, 67, 69–71, 79–81, 87, 89, 92, 98, 113
Alessandrone Perona, Ersilia, 24, 25
Aliberti, Giovanni, 31
Allied landings (in Italy, 1943), 103
Amendola, Giovanni, 28, 29, 51, 68
Anti-feminism, 6
Anti-Semitism, 65, 82, 106, 108
Anti-socialism, 6, 8, 17, 51, 69, 74, 75
Apulia, 11, 73
Aquarone, Alberto, 50–52
Arendt, Hannah, 50, 51
Armed forces (Italian), 50, 52, 85–87, 90
Armistice (Italian, September 1943), 88, 103, 105
Asiago plateau, 40
Auschwitz-Birkenau, 109
Austria, 6, 34, 111
Autarky, 78
Avanti! (socialist newspaper), 8, 18, 32, 35, 45, 70, 75
Avellino, 36
Aventine secession (1924), 14, 16, 41
Axis (Rome-Berlin), 58, 88, 107

B
Badoglio, Pietro, 56, 86, 103
Balbo, Italo, 12, 18, 32
Baldassini, Cristina, 2
Baldissara, Luca, 112
Baldoli, Claudia, 8, 46, 84, 87, 89
Balkans, 6, 71, 83, 84, 88
Banfi, Antonio, 43
Barcelona, 27
Baris, Tommaso, 59, 94
Basel, 28
Belluno, 106
Benedict XV (pope 1914-1922), 7, 23
Ben-Ghiat Ruth, 92
Berezin, Mabel, 92
Bergson, Henri, 30
Berlin, 28, 84
Berlin wall (fall of), 63
Berlusconi, Silvio, 2, 64
Berneri, Camillo, 27, 34, 35
Bianchi, Michele, 12
Bidussa, David, 82, 114
Bissolati, Leonida, 9–11, 17
"Black biennial" (1921-1922), 9–15
Black Brigades (*Brigate nere*, 1944-), 106, 108
Blanqui, August, 75
Bobbio, Norberto, 52, 53
Bocchini, Arturo, 52

Bolshevism
  and Italy, 9, 21
  in Russia, 31
Bolzano, 109
Bombacci, Nicola, 43
Bonaparte Napoleon I, 75
Bonomi, Ivanoe, 11, 12, 21
Bonuglia, Roberto, 31
Bordiga, Amadeo, 32
Boselli, Paolo, 21, 40
Bottai, Giuseppe, 31, 53
Breda factory, Milan, 111
Brescia, 85, 105, 106, 113
British Broadcasting Corporation (BBC), 86, 88

C
Cadorna, Luigi, 45, 69
Calogero, Guido, 53
Calzari Trebeschi Clementina, Foundation (Brescia), 113
Cammarano, Fulvio, 6
Cantimori, Delio, 53
Caporetto (battle of, 1917), 7–9, 40, 46, 69
Castronovo, Valerio, 47, 78
Catholic Church (Vatican)
  and Lateran Pacts, 50, 98
  and peasant unions, 5, 19
  and political struggle, 97
  and the Roman question, 13, 98
Cattaneo, Carlo, 26
Cavagna, Alessandro, 83
Cavarocchi, Francesca, 85
Ceci, Lucia, 2, 14, 97, 98, 113
Ceschin, Daniele, 17, 68, 75
Ceva, Lucio, 86
Chabod, Federico, 40–42, 53
Chessa, Pasquale, 46, 47
Chile, 59
Chiurco, Alberto Giorgio, 18, 32
Christian Democracy (*Democrazia Cristiana*, DC), 63, 64
"Clean hands" (*Tangentopoli*, 1992-), 64
Colarizi, Simona, 63, 64, 86, 89, 92
Cold War, 2, 3, 63–98
Collotti, Enzo, 82–84
Colonialism (fascist), 56–59, 80, 81

Combattentismo (combat culture), 54, 55
Comencini, Luigi, 104
Comintern (Communist International), 19
Communist Party of Italy (*Partito Comunista d'Italia*, PCd'I, 1921-1943), 12, 16
Confino (internal exile), 14
Cooke, Philip, 105
Corfu, 84
Corner, Paul, 91, 93, 94
Corporativism, 78, 79
Corpo truppe volontarie (fascist voluntary groups, Spain 1936-1939), 87
Corradini, Enrico, 30, 67
Corsica, 85
Craxi, Bettino, 64
Cremona, 12, 18, 24
Critica fascista (magazine), 53
Croce, Benedetto, 28, 35, 42, 53, 67
Cuzzi, Marco, 51, 108
Cyrenaica, 57, 81, 89

D
D'Alessandro, Pompeo Leonardo, 89–91
Dalmatia, 6, 9, 31, 69
D'Annunzio, Gabriele, 10, 12, 35, 43, 70
De Ambris, Alceste, 35
De Bono, Emilio, 12
De Felice, Renzo, 18, 32, 34, 39, 41, 42, 44–48, 50–52, 56, 58, 59, 65, 66, 74, 79, 83–85, 89, 90, 92, 107, 112, 113
De Grazia, Victoria, 95, 96
De Luna, Giovanni, 79, 93
De Ninno, Fabio, 90
De Rosa, Gabriele, 39
De Vecchi, Cesare Maria, 12
Deakin, Frederick W., 105, 106
Del Boca, Angelo, 56–58, 80
Del Noce, Augusto, 45, 46
Democratic Party of the Left (*Partito Democratico della Sinistra*, PDS), 63, 64
Deplano, Valeria, 81
Di Figlia, Matteo, 71
Di Nolfo, Ennio, 83

Di Scala Spencer M., 74, 75
Dimitrov, Georgi, 19
Donati, Giuseppe, 24
Dondi, Mirco, 51
Dorso, Guido, 3, 36, 51
Draghi, Mario, 1
Duggan, Christopher, 91, 92
Duranti, Simone, 82

E
East Africa, 57
Ebner, Michael R., 89
Economic depression (1929), 78, 79
Egypt, 57, 85
Elections
  of 1919, 29
  of 1921, 12
  of 1924, 14
  local, 11, 12, 73
  national, 11, 63
Elena, Aga Rossi, 84
Emilia, 109
Enlightenment, 14
Entente, 6, 9, 73
Ertola, Emanuele, 81
Ethiopia, 48, 50, 56–58, 65, 66, 71, 80–84, 87, 103
Etruscans, 83
European civil war, 87, 112
European integration, 63
Exhibition of *romanità*, 83
Exhibition of the fascist revolution, 18, 30
Exile (anti-fascist), 5

F
Fabbri, Luigi, 18
Facta, Luigi, 12, 98
Farinacci, Roberto, 12, 18, 31, 42, 71
Fasci di combattimento (1919), 8
Fascism
  and 1919, 29, 42, 43, 55, 73, 96
  and architecture, 2, 77, 113
  as autobiography of the nation, 24–28
  and the Catholic Church, 50, 82
  and consensus, 1, 48, 56, 59, 67, 82, 90, 111
  and culture, 3, 52–56, 59, 67, 113

  and the economy, 77–80
  and ideology, 1, 25, 34, 47, 52–56, 59, 67, 84
  as a parenthesis, 28, 31, 32, 78, 113
  as a preventive counter-revolution, 112
  and totalitarianism, 19, 49, 51, 52, 59, 72, 112
  and violence, 8, 11, 18, 20, 21, 31, 32, 66, 67, 69–73, 88, 98, 112
  and war, 16, 30, 31, 44, 85–89, 103
  and women, 95–97, 109, 111
Fascist trade unions, 55, 93
Fascist welfare state, 94–95
Female fascist groups (*fasci femminili*), 95
Fenoglio, Beppe, 104
Ferrari, Francesco Luigi, 24
Ferri, Enrico, 35
FIAT Mirafiori, Turin, 111
Fincardi, Marco, 11, 12, 70
Fini, Gianfranco, 63, 64
Fioravanzo, Monica, 107–109
First World War
  and interventionism, 6
  and neutralism, 16
Fiume (Rijeka), 9–12, 43, 70
Florence, 25, 52, 67
Focardi, Filippo, 87, 88, 113
Foot, John, 2
Foreign policy, 20, 29, 33, 57, 65, 73, 82–85, 90
Forza Italia (FI), 64
Fossoli, 109
France, 6, 24, 26, 28, 50, 72, 76, 83, 86, 103, 105
Franco, Francisco, 87
Franzinelli, Mimmo, 17, 31, 36, 42, 46, 69, 70, 72, 73
Fratelli d'Italia (FdI), 1
French revolution, 46, 66
Friuli Venezia Giulia, 6
Fromm, Erich, 42
Fubini, Mario, 53
Futurism, 6, 46, 55, 69, 72

G
Gagliani, Dianella, 108
Gagliardi, Alessio, 59, 78, 79, 92

Galfré, Monica, 31
Galimi, Valeria, 82, 83, 93, 94
Gallerano, Nicola, 87, 90, 94
Galli della Loggia, Ernesto, 104
Ganapini, Luigi, 108
Garibaldi, Giuseppe, 12, 31, 70, 74, 104
Gasparri, Pietro (Vatican Secretary of State), 13, 48
Gebel, 57, 81
Gentile, Emilio, 6, 11, 50, 51, 54–56, 66–69, 71, 72, 74, 76, 88, 91, 97, 113
Gentile, Giovanni, 13, 31, 53, 55, 67, 98
Germany, 2, 6, 26, 34, 43, 44, 46, 47, 50, 58, 66, 84, 86, 90, 107
Germinario, Francesco, 2
Giarrizzo, Giuseppe, 31
Gibelli, Antonio, 67
Giolitti, Giovanni, 6, 11, 16, 21, 23, 29, 36, 41, 44, 47, 57, 67
Giorgi, Chiara, 95
Gissi, Alessandra, 96
Gobetti, Piero, 15, 24–26, 36
Gramsci, Antonio, 3, 16–20, 22, 24, 26, 27, 32, 33, 35, 91, 104
Gramsci foundation (Rome), 112
Granata, Ivano, 72
Grand Council of Fascism, 14
Grandi, Dino, 83, 84
Graziani, Rodolfo, 56, 57, 81
Great Britain, 66, 84, 86
Greece, 85, 87, 88
Gribaudi, Gabriella, 89
Grieco, Ruggero, 22
Gries, 109
Guadalajara (battle of, 1937), 87
Guasco, Alberto, 97, 98
Guerri, Giordano Bruno, 59
Guzzo Domenico, 51

H
Haack, Laurence, 83
Habsburg (monarchy), 6, 17, 26
Historical Institutes for the History of the Resistance, 94
Hitler, Adolf, 46, 50, 66, 83–86, 107, 112, 113
Hollywood, 104

I
Ignazi, Piero, 64
Il Domani d'Italia (newspaper), 24
Il Giornale (newspaper), 44
Il Mondo (liberal newspaper), 28
Il Popolo d'Italia (newspaper), 35, 45, 47, 55, 70, 72, 73, 75, 76
Isnenghi, Mario, 3, 6, 12, 17, 49, 53, 54, 56, 64, 67–70, 75, 85, 91, 93, 97
Italia Contemporanea (academic journal), 40, 58, 65, 96, 105
Italian Communist Party (*Partito Comunista Italiano*, PCI), 18, 19, 63, 64
Italian Encyclopaedia, 53
Italian Nationalist Association (*Associazione Nazionalista Italiana*, ANI), 30
Italian Popular Party (*Partito Popolare Italiano*, PPI), 8, 11, 12, 14, 23, 24, 29, 41, 98
Italian Socialist Party (*Partito Socialista Italiano*, PSI), 8–12, 16, 23, 28, 32, 41, 44, 45, 63, 64, 75, 76, 98
  and maximalism, 22
  and reformism, 22
  and neutralism, 9
Italian Socialist Reformist Party (*Partito socialista riformista italiano*), 9
Italian Social Movement (*Movimento Sociale Italiano*, MSI), 1, 2, 63, 64
Italian Social Republic (*Repubblica Sociale Italiana*, RSI)
  and civil war, 105
  and German occupation of Italy, 98, 103
  and the Holocaust, 65
Italian Society for Labour History (*Società Italiana per la Storia del Lavoro*, SISLav), 77

J
Journal of Modern Italian Studies (academic journal), 91
Justice and Liberty (*Giustizia e Libertà*, GL), 24–26, 36

K

Kienthal, 9
Killinger, Charles, 74, 75
Klinkhammer, Lutz, 107
Knapp, Andrew, 89
Knox, McGregor, 84–86

L

Labanca, Nicola, 80, 81, 84
Labriola, Arturo, 24
Lake Garda, 104
Lanzillo, Agostino, 55
La Rivoluzione liberale (newspaper), 24, 25
La Stampa (newspaper), 16
La Voce (newspaper), 6, 46, 68, 74
Lazio, 43
Lazzari, Costantino, 43
Le Bon, Gustave, 56, 76
League of Nations, 48, 83, 84
Ledeen, Michael, 47
Leed, Eric, 67
Legnani, Massimo, 106
Leninism, 7, 9
Leo XIII (pope 1878-1903), 48
Leonardo (newspaper), 46, 67
Levis Sullam, Simon, 68, 69
Liberalism, Italian, 28, 29
Liberal Italy, 8, 11, 31, 95, 113
Liberation of Italy (1945), 98
Libya, 57, 58, 71
Lipari, 26
Littoria, 48
Livorno, 22
L'Osservatore Romano (newspaper), 13, 98
Lucetti, Gino, 27
L'Unità (newspaper), 20, 68
L'Universale (magazine), 53
Lupo, Salvatore, 92–94
Lussu, Emilio, 13, 19, 26
Luzzatto, Sergio, 64, 76, 77, 80, 81, 90
Lyon theses (1926), 18, 32
Lyttelton, Adrian, 51, 52

M

Maastricht, 63
Malta, 85
Mameli, Goffredo, 104
Manfredi, Marco, 76
Mangoni, Luisa, 53
Marche, 12, 41
Marinetti, Filippo Tommaso, 6, 68, 69
Maritime republics, 70
Matteotti, Giacomo, 14, 20, 44, 50, 71, 104
Maturi, Walter, 53
Mazzantini, Carlo, 104
Mazzini, Giuseppe, 7, 26, 68, 69, 104
Melloni, Alberto, 8
Meloni, Giorgia, 1, 2
Memoria e Ricerca (academic journal), 35, 76
Menotti Serrati, Giacinto, 43
Miccoli, Giovanni, 48, 49, 97
Micheletti Luigi, Foundation (Brescia), 85, 105
Miglioli, Guido, 19, 24, 35
Milan
 and foundation of fascism (1919), 70, 72
 and piazza Fontana massacre (1969), 59
 and the RSI, 108
Millan, Matteo, 67, 71
Milza, Pierre, 46, 47, 70, 74–76, 89, 91
Minesso, Michela, 94, 95
Moscow, 15, 19, 28, 64
Mosse, George, 66
Mussolini, Benito, 2, 8, 11, 13–17, 20, 23–29, 31, 33–36, 42, 44–48, 50, 52, 54–59, 65, 66, 68–77, 79, 82–87, 89–93, 95, 97, 98, 103–105, 107, 108, 111–113
 cult of, 45, 48, 56, 91
 and foundation of fascism, 8
 and socialism, 54, 69, 91
Mussolini, Vittorio, 107

N

National Alliance (*Alleanza Nazionale*, AN), 64
National Association of Combatants (*Associazione Nazionale Combattenti*, ANC), 42
National Fascist Party (Partito *Nazionale Fascista*, PNF), 11, 14, 94

National Institutes for the History of the Resistance, 39
Nationalism, Italian, 68
National Organisation for Maternity and Childhood (*Opera Nazionale Maternità e Infanzia*, ONMI), 93, 97
Nazism (German National Socialism), 2, 44, 65, 66, 104, 113
  and atrocities in Italy, 2
Nenni, Pietro, 22, 27, 29, 30, 33, 40, 72
Nietzsche, Friedrich, 46, 54
Nitti, Francesco Saverio, 26, 29, 31
Non Mollare (newspaper), 25
North Africa, 83, 84
Northern League (*Lega Nord*), 2, 63
Novecento (magazine), 53

O
O'Brien, Paul, 75
Occhetto, Achille, 63
Ojetti, Ugo, 56
Ordine Nuovo (neo-fascist group), 2
Ordine Nuovo (newspaper), 18, 19
Orlando, Vittorio Emanuele, 9, 21, 40
Osti Guerrazzi, Amedeo, 85
Overy, Richard, 89

P
Paci, Deborah, 84, 85
Pact of Steel (1939), 107
Pajetta, Giancarlo, 105, 106
Palla, Marco, 52, 94
Panorama (magazine), 44
Panunzio, Sergio, 55, 75
Papadia, Elena, 76
Papin, Giovanni, 46, 67, 68
Pareto, Vilfredo, 46, 54
Paris, 17, 22–24, 27
Parlato, Giuseppe, 2
Parri, Ferruccio, 40
Passato e presente (academic journal), 84, 94
Passerini, Luisa, 56, 76, 89, 90, 92, 96
Pavolini, Alessandro, 106
Pavone, Claudio, 105, 106
Pes, Alessandro, 80, 81

Pescarolo, Alessandra, 97
Petacco, Arrigo, 59
Petri, Rolf, 78
Pezzino, Paolo, 2
Piazzesi, Mario, 18, 32
Piedmont, 103
Piovene, Guido, 56
Pisanò, Giorgio, 105
Pius XI (pope 1922-1939), 23, 97
Pius XII (pope 1939-1958), 97
Podestà (unelected mayor), 14
Poesio, Camilla, 89
Poland, 107
Pontine marshes, 48, 80
Po valley, 10, 11, 19, 41, 43, 72, 73
Predappio, 77
Pretelli, Matteo, 84
Prezzolini, Giuseppe, 46, 68, 74
Procacci, Giuliano, 40, 43, 44

Q
Quazza, Guido, 39, 47–49, 53, 78

R
Racism, 58, 65, 80–83, 106
Racist laws (1938), 50, 53, 58, 64, 108
Radio Londra, 86
Ragionieri, Ernesto, 15
Ranzato, Gabriele, 112
Rapallo conference, 11
Reagan, Ronald, 47
"Red biennial" (1919-1920), 9–15, 17, 20, 22, 25, 30, 31, 36, 41, 42, 112
Referendum (1946), 104
Republican Fascist Party (*Partito repubblicano fascista*, PRF), 106, 108
Resistance (Italian, 1943-1945), 65, 98, 105
Resta, Giorgio, 2
Revisionism, 59, 66, 83
Revolutionary syndicalism, 46
Ridolfi, Maurizio, 64
Rifondazione Comunista (RC), 63
Rigano, Gabriele, 98
Risiera di San Sabba, 109
Risorgimento, 7, 24–28, 30, 31, 46, 55, 67, 68, 113

Rocco, Alfredo, 6
Rochat, Giorgio, 56–58, 80, 85, 86
Rodogno, Davide, 84
Rodrigo, Javier, 87
Romagna, 75
Rome
   ancient, 70, 79, 83
   march on (28 October 1922), 12, 13, 16
Rosselli, Carlo, 26, 27, 104
Rossi, Ernesto, 25, 72
Rossoni, Aurora, 111
Russia
   and revolution (1917), 25
   Tzarist, 6
Russo, Luigi, 53

S
Sabaudia, 48
Sabbatucci, Giovanni, 45, 46
Salandra, Antonio, 29, 40
Salò, 104
Salvati, Mariuccia, 93, 94
Salvatici, Silvia, 96, 97
Salvatorelli, Luigi, 3, 15, 16, 32, 51
Salvatori, Paola S., 83
Salvemini, Gaetano, 5, 17, 25, 27, 40, 68, 75, 83
Salvini, Matteo, 2
San Sepolcro, 8, 10, 15, 32, 33, 47, 72, 73
Santarelli, Enzo, 19
Sapegno, Natalino, 53
Sapelli, Giulio, 49
Sardinian Action Party (*Partito sardo d'azione*, PdA), 19
Sarfatti, Michele, 82, 109
Savoy (monarchy), 26, 70
Scarpellini, Emanuela, 79
Schiavi, Alessandro, 16, 21
Schirru, Michele, 27
Scoppola, Pietro, 48, 97
Second World War
   and bombing, 88
   and civil war, 105
   and Italian crimes, 87
   and Italian defeat, 1
Segreto, Luciano, 90
Selvaggio (magazine), 53

Settis, Bruno, 79, 80
Sicily, 73, 103
Silone, Ignazio (Tranquilli Secondino), 27, 28, 36
Simonelli, Federico Carlo, 70
Slovenia, 7
Snodi (academic journal), 64
Socialism, Italian
   and charismatic leaders, 35, 45
   and defeat by fascism, 19
   and peasant organisations, 13
   and trade unions, 16, 20, 23, 44
Soffici, Ardengo, 68
Sonnino, Sidney, 40
Sorel, Georges, 30, 46, 54, 55, 72, 76
Southern question, 27, 28
South Tyrol, 6
Soviet Union, 50, 63–65
Spain, 27, 34, 71, 87
Spanish Civil War, 27, 48, 66, 87
Special Tribunal for State Security, 14, 71
Speranzini, Giuseppe, 24
Spinosa, Antonio, 59
Spirito, Ugo, 55
Squadrismo (fascist), 11, 18, 33, 43, 46, 67, 71, 73
St. Paul, 48
Stalin, Joseph, 19, 50
Stelliferi, Paola, 96, 97
Sternhell, Zeev, 72
Strategy of tension, 51
Studi Storici (academic journal), 59, 66, 78, 90, 91, 94, 95, 97
Sturzo, Luigi, 8, 14, 23, 41, 98
Switzerland, 9, 13, 28

T
Tamaro, Attilio, 31, 39
Tarchi, Marco, 2
Tasca, Angelo, 17, 20, 23, 27–30, 32–35, 41
Teshale, Tibebuereign, 113
Third International, 19, 23, 36
Togliatti, Palmiro, 15, 19, 22, 23, 33, 34, 113
Toniolo, Gianni, 78
Tranfaglia, Nicola, 59, 84
Traniello, Francesco, 48

Traverso, Enzo, 112
Trentin, Silvio, 72
Trentino, 6, 74
Treves, Claudio, 7, 22, 44
Treviglio, 111
Trieste, 109
Troilo, Simona, 83
Tunisia, 85
Turati, Filippo, 16, 21, 22, 26, 29, 40, 43, 44
Turi, Gabriele, 98
Turin
  and August 1917, 8, 69
  and Congress of the PPI, 98
  and factory councils, 18, 44
Tuscany, 11, 41, 73
TV Sorrisi e canzoni (magazine), 44

U
Umbria, 11, 41
Unitary Socialist Party (*Partito socialista unitario*, PSU), 44
United Nations (UN), 88
United States of America (USA), 9
University fascist Groups (*Gruppi universitari fascisti*, GUF), 93
Ustasha (Croatian), 88
Utopia (newspaper), 75

V
Vacca, Giuseppe, 19, 20
Valeri, Nino, 39, 41–43
Vecchi, Ferruccio, 69
Vendramini, Ferruccio, 106
Venice, 104
Ventrone, Angelo, 67–69
Ventura, Andrea, 72, 73
Verona, 106, 109
Versaille (treaty), 9, 43, 83
Vezzosi, Elisabetta, 97
Victor Emmanuel III of Savoy (king of Italy 1900-1946), 13, 50
Vidotto, Vittorio, 84
Villari, Francesco, 47
Vittorio, Veneto (battle of, 1918), 87, 107
Vivarelli, Roberto, 70
Volpe, Gioacchino, 5, 17, 18, 30, 31, 53

W
War in History (academic journal), 87
Willson, Perry, 95, 96
Wilson, Woodrow, 9

Y
Yugoslavia, 9, 85, 87, 88

Z
Zeno-Zencovich, Vincenzo, 2
Zewde, Barhu, 113
Zibordi, Giovanni, 33, 34
Zimmerwald, 9
Zurich, 28

SPRINGER NATURE

GPSR Compliance

The European Union's (EU) General Product Safety Regulation (GPSR) is a set of rules that requires consumer products to be safe and our obligations to ensure this.

If you have any concerns about our products, you can contact us on ProductSafety@springernature.com

In case Publisher is established outside the EU, the EU authorized representative is:

Springer Nature Customer Service Center GmbH
Europaplatz 3
69115 Heidelberg, Germany

The manufacturer's authorised representative in the EU is Springer Nature Customer Service Centre GmbH, Europaplatz 3, 69115 Heidelberg, Germany. If you have any concerns regarding our products, please contact ProductSafety@springernature.com

Printed and bound by CPI Group (UK) Ltd, Croydon, CR0 4YY

23/03/2026

02076394-0012